∽ SALAMANDER

SALAMANDER

SELECTED POEMS OF ROBERT MARTEAU

TRANSLATED BY ANNE WINTERS

PRINCETON UNIVERSITY PRESS
PRINCETON, NEW JERSEY

Copyright © 1979 by Princeton University Press

Published by Princeton University Press, Princeton, New Jersey
In the United Kingdom: Princeton University Press, Guildford, Surrey

ALL RIGHTS RESERVED

Library of Congress Cataloging in Publication Data will be found on the last
printed page of this book

The Lockert Library of Poetry in Translation is supported by a bequest from
Charles Lacy Lockert (1888-1974).

This book has been composed in linotype Times Roman

Clothbound editions of Princeton University Press books are printed on acid-free
paper, and binding materials are chosen for strength and durability.

Printed in the United States of America by Princeton University Press,
Princeton, New Jersey

⌒TABLE OF CONTENTS

∽WORKS BY ROBERT MARTEAU

POETRY

Royaumes   Paris, Editions du Seuil (1962)
Ode Numéro 8   Paris, Syrinx (1965)
Travaux sur la terre   Paris, Editions du Seuil (1966)
Sibylles (drawings by Singier)   Paris, Galanis (1971)
Hélène (lithographs by Minaux)   Paris, Editions Sauret (1974)
Atlante   Montréal, Hexagone (1976)
Traité du blanc et des teintures (embossments by Tremblay)   Montréal, Editions
   Erta (1978)

NOVELS

Des chevaux parmi les arbres   Paris, Editions du Seuil (1968)
Pentecôte   Paris, Gallimard (1973)

OTHERS

El Cordobés (photographs by Lucien Clergue)   Paris, La Jeune Parque (1965)
Chagall sur la terre des dieux (lithographs by Chagall)   Paris, Editions Mazo
   (1966)
Les Vitraux de Chagall (album)   Paris, Editions Mazo (1972)
The Stained Glass Windows of Chagall   New York, Tudor (1973)
Les Ateliers de Chagall (lithographs)   Paris, Mourlot (1976)
La Voix sous la pierre (poems translated from the Serbo-Croatian of
   Miodrag Pavlovitch)   Paris, Gallimard (1970)
L'Œil ouvert (essays on art)   Montréal, Quinze (1978)
Les Livres de Hogg (poems translated from the English of Barry
   Callaghan)   Montréal, Quinze (1978)

⌒ACKNOWLEDGMENTS

I should like to acknowledge my gratitude to the Camargo Foundation in Cassis, France, where the greater number of these translations were completed; and to its director, Russell Young. I am grateful as well to the French poet Michel Deguy and to Professor A. James Arnold of the University of Virginia, who encouraged my project.

My work would have been extraordinarily difficult without the sympathetic consultation and advice of Robert Marteau himself. I should also like to thank my husband, Alan Williamson, for his help in typing the manuscript and for many invaluable suggestions.

My translation of the section of *Travaux pour un bûcher* was originally published in *Sumac*, Spring, 1969. The translation of *Circé* appeared in *Pequod*, Summer, 1975, and that of *Royauté* in *Poetry*, April, 1979. The translations are reprinted here by the kind permission of the editors of these magazines.

~ SALAMANDER

~INTRODUCTION

Robert Marteau's poems move continually between the barest, most irreducible vision of the creative act—"I am only this stone where the blackberry flowers"—and a resonant, seething universe where creation seems to be going on under every leaf, at every moment.

> Then I will have
> only the word itself to offer the woodman
> or the weaving woman who holds
> with a single strand the vulture and the dance
> and the kid to its milky jug
> and on the fig one black and yellow wasp
> darkening the altar with false wax.

In many ways his work finds its truest analogies in painting, for the poems glisten with fugitive detail, with what the eye has netted. In their emphasis on light and perception, they recall Vermeer, an artist with whom Marteau feels strong affinities. Vermeer's paintings always have at their center a moment of stillness and light, and usually a contemplative human figure—an astronomer, an artist, or a woman sewing, weighing pearls, reading a letter. Behind these luminous annunciations the world opens out into maps and windows, and space fills up with the impedimenta of living: mops, the servant's clog, a paintbrush. The radiant centers in Marteau's poetry are similarly heightened by their immersion in the *pâte*, the quiddity, of everyday life.

His vocabulary is correspondingly dense. It bristles with botanical and nautical technicalities, with laborers' tools: the baker's shovel, the countrywoman's washing-club, terms relating to tanning and carpentry —even for the French these are recondite. Yet it is with these tools, the poems imply, that the world is seized, shaped, fashioned—all work echoes the original work of creation. As Marteau explains in a prefatory note to his collection *Travaux sur la terre*: "True knowledge is continually lost, and perpetually man devotes himself to the quest of that impossible moment when speech coincides with the Word, the wine with the cup. The body of the god is forever rent and dispersed. All works are efforts towards reassembling and resembling that essential model, whose emanations we perceive but which remains separate from us because of our limited degree of vision."

If all works recall the Great Work, so are all locations potentially imaginative foci. Words for *place* abound: *lieu, arène, aire, terrain.* Any

3

site where the encounter with the absolute is imminent: the bull ring at five o'clock, the street of a Spanish city at dawn, the heart of the forest, may become the spiritual center of the universe. In Pascal's phrase, "C'est une sphère dont le centre est partout, la circonférence nulle part."

Another initially striking feature of Marteau's poetry is its velocity. As one admiring French reviewer, himself a poet, described it: "The reader . . . suddenly wonders if his reason is giving way under this avalanche of telescoped images." It is the profusion of juxtapositions, seeming dissimilarities joined by the urgency of the poet's imagination, that caused readers of Marteau's first two books to comment on their Baroque quality. As in the poetry of Donne, say, or Gongora, an important influence on Marteau's work, vivid equations are continually forming between sacred and profane terms, between abstractions and particularities. Consider Marteau's sonnet on the seventeenth-century Spanish painter Zurbaran, which focuses on a piece of "starlike bread" (perhaps one of the large cleaved rolls in Zurbaran's paintings). These are the last six lines:

> Whether the same white star prints the coal
> Or whether night's waters take it, return it
> We see that the soul's mirrors petrify
>
> That which time would corrupt and destroy
> Meditating on threshing floors, the Apostles and Christ
> Clothe their church in asbestos robes

Beneath these bewilderingly rapid transitions lies an implicit but precise metaphorical structure. Zurbaran's sculptural coolness and concentration of spiritual presence suggest the eucharistic mystery, which in turn resembles that of bread-making itself, in which the energy of the sun and of coal, of bakers and threshers, are brought to rigidity in asbestos-clad ovens. It is also interesting that according to the *Golden Legend*, Epiphany celebrates the appearance of the star to the Magi, and is observed on the same day as Phagophany (the miracle of Christ's multiplication of the loaves).

In Marteau's more recent poems, those published in the middle seventies, we find the same condensation of allusions, but the language is more abstract, the images are noted with hieroglyphic brevity. Sketching out a compressed and secret cosmogony, the poet's imagination in *Traité du blanc et des teintures* seems to mark the paper as lightly and rapidly as a Zen poet-painter's inkbrush:

> As yet the world has only one voice,
>   but the propagated wave
> in moving away from the point grows heavy,

from effluvia forming the river
    as well as all states
according to amplitude and frequency.

    Through the vertical
the other salt here divides,
    the gods' single tear,
for after all is life, death, and the seasons.

The voice, the creative *fiat*, the "word to the woodman," is always offered anew in Marteau's poems. It is true that they also contain a strong elegiac strain, for to each generation it seems that Hopkins' "dearest freshness deep down things," Yeats' "ceremony of innocence," is more inaccessible. Yet from Marteau's early poem "Work for a Pyre" on, it has been clear that for him this withdrawal, like the rending and recovery of the god, is a necessary part of the rhythm of creation and consciousness. Like the salamander, emblem of transmutation and imperishability, the Word lives on in the fire which consumes it:

    The holy flames
Which rinse to gold the matter of mountain clefts,
Which are themselves the straw where salamanders nest,
Which no wind reverses but the Pentecost bends back,
Which survive the wood, thrust down the serpent's
    Pythian ring,
The same which clothe in blue the plaster madonnas,
Which are the sky's navel and which are seen in the
    mirror of the gods,
The same which consume the pyre
Where already Troy is transfigured.

II

Robert Marteau was born in 1925 in a village within the *forêt domaniale* and game preserve of Chizé, near the border of Charente and Poitou in southwestern France. His poems often evoke this landscape: particularly the rivers and marshes of Charente, which mingle ocean and pasturage, orchards, vineyards, and milch-cows. The neighboring *bocage* of Poitou is curiously untidy for a French landscape; its *allées* of shade trees are less than rigorously pollarded, and the haystacks stand almost as high as the red-tiled farmhouses. In the villages within this area, of which Marteau has written in his novel *Des Chevaux parmi les arbres*, and which lay on the medieval pilgrimage route to Compostela, are many exquisite small Romanesque churches. The young Marteau was familiar with their curious façades, carved with classical acanthus leaves,

5

fish-tailed centaurs, and fabulous oriental monsters. Carved among these, and among biblical scenes, are the traditional signs of the Zodiac and Occupations of the Months, portrayed with rural realism and with particularly vivid hunting scenes. He thus received as part of his Poitevin inheritance a world-view which held "with a single strand" elements of paganism, Christianity and the telling detail of everyday labor.

Eventually the isolation of provincial life would lead Marteau to continue his preparation for his now clearly sensed poetic career in the icy discomfort of post-Liberation Paris. But the poems written there, even years later, blend spiritual themes with dense and fantastic rural imagery:

> Let the seed die, and the fading leaves
> And beanstalks rot; for the bull

> The goat and the other beasts that wind through the sky
> Are massing behind the clouds (as we might gather mushrooms
> Or sorb-apples) the fodder of shattered stars
> On which the sun grows fat.
>
> ("Charente")

When Marteau was asked, on accepting the Prix René Laporte for his first collection of poems in 1963, what had been "the great event of his life," he answered: "Seeing Claudel's *Le Soulier de satin* performed, shortly after my arrival in Paris in 1944." He was reading and writing intensively, in small rooms in the Latin Quarter, composing and throwing away "des kilos de poèmes." (More than a decade of this practice may help explain the unusually even excellence of his first book, *Royaumes*.) He took a few courses at the *Institut d'études hispaniques*, and studied English as well; but his true universities, as he later remarked, were painting, travel, and most particularly alchemy, in which he had developed a strong interest. He read among many others the works of the contemporary Adept Fulcanelli, and also discovered the volumes of Emile Soldi-Colbert de Beaulieu on the traditional significance of symbols, which became for him the *summa* of symbolical studies. We will return to Marteau's interest in esotericism at a later point, for it was to influence strongly his thinking and imagery.

His poems were now appearing in reviews, first in *Les Cahiers du Sud*, then in *Les Lettres nouvelles* and in *Esprit*. His interest in Spain grew steadily over the years, and he began visiting it as often as possible. He immersed himself in the poetry of Gongora, in the great painting of the *siglo de oro*; and he followed the bullfight closely, for some years rarely missing the Pamplona festival.

Perhaps the greatest gift of Paris itself to the poet was its art. Like many French poets from the nineteenth century on—from Baudelaire through Apollinaire—Marteau has been deeply involved with contemporary painting. When he joined the Parisian review *Esprit*, his own *chronique* was given over to essays on art, and he has lived more in artistic than in literary circles in the city. For many years he earned his living mainly by work involved in some way with art—directing seminars, directing and writing films on contemporary artists, organizing exhibitions.

Painting for Marteau is one of the arenas, as is the bullfight, for the central *aventure*, or quest, of the eye and spirit. That it is also intimately related to his own poetic practice may be illustrated by a passage from his book *Les Vitraux de Chagall*. Speaking of the actual process, the *poieîn* as it were, of painting, he comments:

> "All things are white in God's hands before they are colored," says a very ancient alchemical text. To color and to engrave: it is by this movement that man makes the creation visible, signifying at the same time his identity with the Cosmos and his difference from it, indissociable from the act of knowing.

In the French, "colored" and "to color" are *teintes* and *teindre*. The verb can mean either to color or to prepare a chemical tincture; in alchemy *teintures* may also indicate the stages of preparation and the series of colors that succeed each other in the Great Work. All of Marteau's writings on art make it clear that, as the Québecois poet Fernand Ouellette has put it, Marteau "enters a museum because a museum is first and foremost one of the sites of the 'enchanted forest.' "

Marteau's involvement in art has not slackened since his removal to Québec some years ago. The long poem *Traité du blanc et des teintures* (1978) was published in Montréal in collaboration with the artist Gérard Tremblay, as previous books had appeared with drawings or lithographs by Bertholle, Singier, Minaux in Paris. Some of his recent work also evokes the New World; in the embattled western land of Québec, the forest realm of seventeenth-century French, Marteau feels, curiously, a sense of return. As he said in a recent statement in the Canadian magazine *Ellipse* about his arrival in Québec: "I was rediscovering my origins, rallying eagerly to the patrimony, and, as a poet, was passionately learning to know my homeland: this mother tongue which from the womb is constantly haggled over and threatened."

III

"All things descend from the same seed, and originally all were born of the same mother." This maxim of Basil Valentinus, the fifteenth-century monk of Erfurt, restates the basic principle of alchemy. *Omnia in unum*, the unity of matter; and thence the cosmic analogies (between planets and minerals, the four elements and the four bodily humours, the macrocosm of the universe and the microcosm of the human body). Thence also the potential for infinite metamorphoses (the generation of metals) and for infinite sympathies: Baudelaire's *correspondances*. It is through these analogies that the world, according to the Hermetic cosmogony, recalls its unfallen state, when the Garden was still enclosed in the mind of the Creator. There the energies of plants, animals, and all created objects coexisted interchangeably, still resonant from the initial impulse of Creation. The Fall is seen as the organic next phase of creative expansion: from primary universe to manifest world, to generation, ramification, conscious distinctness. The serpent, the undulant line of creativity, now appears upright on the Tree of Knowledge. Like the serpents on Hermes' caduceus, in this position he symbolizes the demiurge of articulation and revelation: the Logos, which from the beginning has mediated between the two worlds.

In the largest sense, the alchemist attempts to reconstitute that fallen unity, to restore nature and man to their Edenic state. The Philosopher's Stone, far from being sought principally as a source of gold, is itself the Universal Medicine, the Elixir of Life; the projection on base metal to produce gold being merely the final test of its readiness. In Robert Marteau's words, the basic goal of alchemy is "to conquer, or rather reanimate, matter, which has fallen asleep; to awaken its inner waves, so that it may again become that living, vibratory, celestial matter, the very light emanated from the Principle. . . ." To recognize the significance for Marteau's poetry of this goal (and of many other alchemical doctrines touched on in this discussion), it is important to bear in mind that alchemy is not alone in its powers of reconstitution. The old treatises call it the Celestial Agriculture, and the Great Art or Great Work; all essentially creative, self-perfecting, generative acts may be seen as quickening the vibration still latent in the manifest world.

> The folded wave
> throbs among lips and petals,
> it baffles the Fall, and delights
> in the throat, in the shell,
> and in the play of knees.

Inasmuch as alchemy strives to recover a primary, purified experience, to "baffle the Fall," it finds its paradigm in Christ's passion, as well as in the quests of mythical heroes, the initiatory rites (many elements of the ancient mystery religions passed into the Hermetic books), and ultimately in the workings of nature.

The fabrication of the Philosopher's Stone also traditionally entails the exploration and development of the self. The alchemist first purifies himself and seeks out the advice of an Adept or of treatises; then he searches for the *materia prima* of his work, which he must personally select. (These preparations may be compared to the initial ascesis of the mysteries, with the Sibyl's advice to Aeneas and his preliminary search for the Golden Bough.) Later this matter, the *terre noire*, will be placed in a vessel (the "closed vase" or "philosophic egg"), in the alchemist's furnace. Its transformations begin with a phase of dissolution and putrefaction. This important stage is in turn comparable with the death of the vegetation god, with the underworld passages in the myths, and with the initiates' descent into the subterranean labyrinths at Eleusis. In the Eleusinian initiations, it was the Great Mother who dominated this phase, although the initiate identified himself with Dionysus. It is the vision of her procreative mysteries that offers reintegration and rebirth; she presides over the sacrifice.

> Above, the Mother savors the early froth
> Of an August vintage, below they let fall
> Petals of spikenard and jasmine on his eyes.
> ("For the Twelfth Anniversary
> of the Death of Manolete")

But the Mother not only presides, in a sense she is herself the mineral worked upon; the *materia* itself is considered one with the *Mater*, and with the Black Virgin of the medieval crypts.

In the phase that gradually succeeds the *œuvre au noir*, the alchemist will see his matter slowly reconstitute itself and lighten to the purest white. But the treatises stress that he must continue to tend his furnace and regulate his fire. The white phase will eventually be followed by a higher level of purification, reddening, intensity; this in turn is followed at the end by the long-sought absolute synthesis. If the alchemical search for truth and transmutation is often compared to that of lovers, then this final phase constitutes the alchemical wedding, at once the union and transcendence of the male and female principles. The result of their union is the Philosopher's Stone, that stone which is also a powder, which is identified with Christ and with the return to an eternal present.

It will be clear at this point that the alchemical treatises, the novice's "Ariadne's threads," are themselves mines of imagery and allegory. Their secrecy also corresponds to the ellipses and obscurity of Robert Marteau's poetic voice: like Virgil's Sibyl he speaks *obscuris vera involvens*. But alchemy has above all provided Marteau with a rigorous, inclusive ideal of poetic practice. As he has stressed, quoting Antonin Artaud, in all alchemical work the sublime is attained only after "a minute and exacerbating pulverization of all insufficiently refined, insufficiently matured forms. For it is in the very principle of alchemy not to permit the spirit to take flight except after passing through all the canalizations, all the basements and strata, of matter as it exists, and after having doubly redone this work. . . ." It is to just such a rigorous sifting through of *actuality* that Marteau's work owes its density and conviction.

"Charente, Again," from Marteau's first collection, clearly exemplifies the interdependence in his work of alchemy, poetic technique, and personal experience. As its title suggests, the poem itself is a "doubling" of the preceding "Charente." This country is the poet's own *terre noire*, and through evocations of its seasons and rural occupations, he struggles toward a formulation of its essence. The sequence of images follows the major stages of the overall alchemical injunction *Solve et coagula* ("Dissolve and coagulate"). In the first lines the landscape is obscurely decomposing: "Strewn on bundles of rotting brushwood." In the third and fourth stanzas, the fermented mass is distilled, "transmuted into spirit," until the alchemical whiteness appears ("On the ermine's track / A bundle of whetted arrows / Trails from alcohol's frosty gloves"). Distillation is followed by a further purifying procedure, sublimation ("All thought / Disappears in the presence of prayer"). There is no laboratory-manual fidelity; but we sense that refinement in the imagination may not be less subtle than in the retort. Certainly at the close the poet has restored Charente, his gift and his given, to its most crystalline, irreducible form:

> Black seed, homeland and powder blown in my eyes,
> These make my furnace, where the Fall and windfallen
> Images turn into truth.

The language of the alchemical treatises, as well as the actual procedures, is reflected in Marteau's poetry—particularly in the bewildering fusions of allegory and laboratory terminology. Images themselves carry an unusual amount of information in the treatises; one, the celebrated *Mutus Liber*, consists of plates only. Here is a typical passage from the seventeenth-century *Principles of Philalethus*:

> To obtain our tincture, however, this is not yet enough; the water of our lake must boil with the ashes of the tree of Hermes. I advise you to boil it continually, day and night, so that during the workings of our stormy sea, the celestial nature may rise and the terrestrial nature descend. . . . Precipitate nothing in the hope of an early harvest, I mean of our Work, but labor confidently for at least fifty days, and you will see the beak of the crow of good omen. . . . When you perceive it [the first signs of blackness] you may conclude that your body is destroyed, that is to say reduced to

a living spirit; and your spirit is dead, that is to say coagulated with the body.

This text is, of course, an exact description of laboratory procedures—but in the way that the opening of *Taureaux dans Bayonne*, for example, describes the environs of the bullring and the combat of the bull and matador.

A final point on the relation of alchemy to myth. For Marteau, alchemy offers the key to a deeper symbolism common to all myths and religions. It is "the spring of the myths, and speaks their language in a sacred, symbolic and universal tongue." Thus he is predisposed to base the structure of his long poems—as Eliot, Pound, and Crane did in English—on montage, merging contemporary episodes with more than one level of mythic action. The forest of the loggers in *Travaux pour un bûcher*, for instance, is seen as one with all sacred forests:

> We can hear a faint lopping of branches
> Because the wind stands strongly from the wooded regions;
> The forests of Pharaoh, and Broceliande, and the wood
>   of prophetic leaves,
> Are leveled, the trunks are in piles, the bundles
>   tied and gathered. From labyrinth to labyrinth
> The corn-ricks in barnyards raise their yellow bells
> From which, at a distance, cyclists see swallows escaping.

In the heart of the forest, French countrymen, their chores described in intimate detail, mingle their features with those of classical heroes. At times they seem to be Aeneas' men, wandering through the *antiquam silvam* cutting trees for their dead comrade's pyre. But Homer ultimately predominates, and at the close it is Patrocles who "when all is fallen, aspires to the flame."

The long poem *Circé*, also translated in this selection, superimposes two myths upon a site both classical and modern. The poem was written on the Yugoslavian island of Krk (one of many that claim Homer's sorceress *Kirkē*), when Marteau was translating the Serbian poet Miodrag Pavlovitch. It is now a summer resort where the old rural life scarcely survives, and the closing section of the poem is a response to the death of a child killed by a tourist's car during Marteau's stay on the island. The main *aventure* is Odysseus' interlude with Circe, who will equip him for his underworld descent and his return to Ithaca. His wanderings are counterpointed by allusions to Theseus' escape from the Minotaur and labyrinth. Here the Minotaur seems to recall the descent of modern European civilization from the union of Europa and the god-bull. But the mythic energies thus generated have shrunk to a trickle in

11

the modern world glimpsed in this poem. The swine of Circe—who have traded their humanity for the peace of a pigsty—express Marteau's most ferocious view thus far of contemporary life.

The story of Theseus links this poem to the many Marteau has written about the bullfight, for the legend is thought to derive from the ancient Cretan bull-dance, familiar from the Knossos fresco-painting. The dance may have been a propitiation of a chthonic deity, the god of earthquakes, earth-shaker Poseidon; at any rate in most versions it is stressed that Theseus offers himself voluntarily as a sacrificial victim, then triumphs over his death. Marteau's *corrida* symbolism stresses the elements in the bullfight which are parallel with vegetation rites (the first bullfights are held in March, at the time of the first work in the fields) and with the Passion of Christ. It is also interesting that the labyrinth itself (which appears on Virgil's Cumaean cave door, and was carved by the medieval builders on the cathedral crossings of Chartres, Rheims, Amiens and elsewhere), is a traditional emblem of the *Grand Œuvre*. The following passage, from *Taureaux dans Bayonne*, is addressed to the matadors:

> Dressed in rigid vestments,
> The cornea white as gouache,
> Feet joined, you advance on the seismograms' swell.
>> At the limits of Eden, you relieve the angelic
>> guard: Persephone flees, and the bride of
>> Minos invokes the white flower of the narcissus.
> All powers are placed in your hands: you bind and
>> unbind the graces and forces;
> Subject to your gestures, the waters cascade and
>> thunder. . . . You bow! . . . The mules drag off the
>> bull, but death is so lovely he follows it up
>> the silk ladder.

Few themes lie nearer the center of Marteau's poetic thought than that of the transcendence—transmutation, perhaps—of death. It is the central theme of alchemy as well: the transmutation of the corruptible, the accidental, into a radiant permanence. For Patrocles, the pyre. For Manolete, the perfumed flowers; for the bull, the entry into the permanence of ritual. If *Circé*, as I have said, takes up what is almost a twentieth-century tradition of basing works of art on the *Odyssey*, it is also a lament for the loss of such myths, the disappearance of deeply felt ritual. Our century can offer the pointlessly slain child neither ritual oils and perfumes nor the *stele*, the upright stone signifying articulate mourning and the possibility of resurrection. We lack the auspices of Hermes-Thoth, the Word whom the serpents, intermediaries between the worlds, and the recording reed must both obey. But the closing lines carry the implication that the quest for chthonic passage and return, like the request for articulacy, becomes its own answer. For Marteau the poem itself has always been a symbolic stone, a tincture of irreducible life.

At the end of the book the reader will find brief notes on the following poems: "Charente," "Lozère," "Mélusine," "For the Twelfth Anniversary of the Death of Manolete," "Veronica," "Black Banderillas," "*Faena de Capa*," "Ode Number 8."

I

FROM
Royaumes
(1962)

ROYAUTE

La nuit sans bouche, la nuit sans plume; la nuit de poudre noire et des
    ombres qui bougent;
La nuit des cavernes, la nuit d'un seul coup de fusil et d'aucun chant
    de coq,
La nuit compacte, dans ses glaces prenant les anges du combat, et la
    murène aux taches de venin;
La nuit de verre, la nuit sans faille,
Du bout de ton fuseau, bergère, tu la brises . . . Tu la couvres de dentelle
    et de fils . . . D'une Lorraine de gelée blanche, tu te lèves . . . La
    Champagne s'éveille dans le bouillon de tes jupes; et l'Artois dans
    ses prismes sépare les couleurs.

Les Grandes Compagnies descendent sur l'Espagne;
Elles sentent le harnais, le cuir, la morve des chevaux.
Dans la Gascogne, entre les haies de maïs, les oies trompent le silence.
    Goût de sable, goût d'œillet,
Sous un ciel frangé de noir
Comme une huître.

Epée de basalte
Dans la forêt de sapins!
La neige sous l'écorce et Pampelune morte parmi les truites . . .
Le vent se fige sur l'autel et les anges de plâtre et la Sainte Famille
Sur la haute marée, sur leur mâture de bois,
Tendent des toiles bleu marine et s'en vont à l'aveugle
Ainsi que tout et même ces rues sous les fanaux
Qui sont comme les planches d'une nef.

Malte!
Tunis!
Cités noires où le soleil crucifié règne en maître
Bien qu'écartelé, à coups de mail et de coins,
Tenu sur les quatre feuilles de la peste.

Sur les poitrines, ces croix;
Dans les mains, ces clochettes;

⌒ROYALTY

The night of no mouth, the featherless; the night of black powder and
    moving shadows;
Night of caverns, night with one rifle shot and no cockcrow,
The night compact, with angels of combat caught in its mirrors, and
    the moray spotted with venom;
The night made of faultless glass,
One tap of your distaff, shepherdess, and it's shattered . . . .
    You wrap it in lace and in threads. . . . From a Lorraine of white
    frost, you arise. . . . The land of Champagne awakes in your
    welling skirts; the Artois deep in its prisms divides the colors.

The great bands of mercenaries sweep down on Spain;
Reeking of harness, of leather, the streaming nostrils of horses.
Among the cornrows of Gascony, geese betray the silence. Tang of
    sand, tang of pinks,
Under a sky fringed with black
Like an oyster.

Basalt sword
In the forest of firs!
Snow under the bark and Pamplona dead among trout. . . .
The wind congeals on the altar and the plaster angels and the Holy
    Family
Out on the high tide, on their wooden masts,
Spread sea-blue sails and then set out blindly
As everything else and even the streets in the lantern light
Are like the planks of a ship.

Malta!
Tunis!
Black cities where the crucified sun reigns as master
Though quartered by blows of the wedge and sledgehammer,
Though held high on the quatrefoil of the plague.

These crosses on their chests;
These small bells in their hands;

Ces bubons sur les lèvres, et ce rêve d'un seul désert
Plein d'os bien blancs et propres.

Bergers des morts
Qui fouettez devant les vertes giboulées
Vos troupeaux de cigognes; bergers dans le vent,
Le visage cinglé par la crinière des chevaux;
Maîtres des faucons,
Lieutenants, cavaliers, trappeurs,
La reine tisse, vous brodez sur la haute laine
L'image précieuse de vos courses. L'autour sur le gant de cuir un instant
       s'attache;
Il flamboie, et l'herbe bouge et le voilà suivant la courbure du ciel, et
       puis dans la poussière, la plume et le sang.
Les troupeaux transhument: une odeur de laiterie traverse les portes de
       madriers. . .
Et le roi regarde son royaume
Et ses grandes fermes qui voyagent. Il s'en va dans son chariot de
       comédie. Il dort sur ses peaux de bœufs et d'antilopes,
Et il entend les jurons des bouviers et les bâtons qu'ils cassent dessous
       les roues.
Ah! royaume. Et partout ces princes capricieux qui coupent son sommeil
       de fêtes trop violentes. Lui qui gouvernait les yeux fermés,
Voilà qu'on l'éveille: alors tout se fragmente, se morcelle; il n'est plus
       prince que d'un coin de terre
Que limite à l'ouest le marais, à sa gauche un bois de châtaigniers.
On tend son arc, la flèche vole ou bien c'est le tiercelet: entre les cornes
       des bœufs, une sarcelle vient s'abattre.
Derrière nous, les neiges pleines de grelots et de lamas. Nous entrons
       dans le pays des Celtes: douze pierres sur le ciel gravent les routes
       astrales; sur le trèfle blanc, une barque; mais la mer elle-même se
       couvre d'un bruit de fenaison . . . Faneuses!
Vos râteaux éparpillent la lumière. De vos fronts de plume, poussant les
       marées (et vos yeux, lentement, de sombre vin!)
Bœufs!
Aux bourrelets de vos pattes traînant des isthmes,
Abordant des contrées de varech et de vastes moulins,
De grands empires, des terres gavées de sang,
Bœufs! devant vous forçant les portes nocturnes,
L'éventail des poutres et des tornades—

These boils on their lips, and this dream of a single desert
Full of very clean white bones.

Shepherds of the dead
Who lash their flocks of storks before
The sudden green showers; shepherds in the wind,
Their faces slashed by the horses' manes;
Falcon-masters,
Lieutenants, horsemen and trappers,
The queen is weaving, and on the long wool you embroider
The rare images of your journeys. One instant the goshawk clings on
    the leather glove;
He flames up, the grass sways and he goes curving along with the sky,
    and then in the dust, the plumage and blood.
The flocks change their pastures: a smell of milking comes through the
    thick-beamed doors. . . .
And the king considers his kingdom
And his great travelling farms. He goes off in his stage-chariot, sleeps
    on his oxhides and antelope skins,
And he hears the drovers cursing, the poles cracking under the wheels.
Ah! kingdom. And on all sides these capricious princes breaking into his
    sleep with their violent feast days. He who governed eyes closed,
Now they're waking him up: then everything fragments, falls into
    parcels; he's only prince of a small spot of earth
Bounded on the west by the marsh, on his left by a forest of chestnuts.
The bow is bent, the arrow flies or the falcon: a teal hurtles down
    between the two ox-horns.
Behind us, the snows full of small bells and llamas. We enter the land
    of the Celts: twelve stones on the sky mark the astral paths; a boat
    on white clover; but the sea itself is wrapped in a sound of hay-
    making. . . . Women tossing the hay!
Your rakes strew the sunlight. And with your feathery foreheads,
    pushing the tides (and your eyes, slowly, with their somber wine!)
Oxen!
Trailing isthmuses from your pasterns,
Touching on regions of seaweed, enormous mills,
Great empires and lands gorged with blood,
Oxen! Forcing the nocturnal gates before you,
The fan of tornadoes and timbers—

C'est l'ouest:
La Vendée plus douce qu'un plumage,
Les îles dans la pourpre des joncs.

Voici les terres spirituelles, les pluies tellement tristes. Voici la tourbière
    et le mufle des bêtes,
Le chien, et le ponceau que le vent soulève,
Là-bas, entre les haies, où la pluie encore, bien que menue,
S'acharne contre un bruit de chariots et de cloches; contre un parfum de
    tilleul. . . Et la dernière étoile
Vacille sur sa tige de graisse.

Pays! je m'agenouille, je touche l'herbe!
Je compte tes os; j'aime ton odeur de vin et de tabac,
De poils, de fourrure, d'aile mouillée,
Et les charrois d'hiver dans la noirceur des forêts,
Et le cor et la conque marine et les phares qui tournent.
J'aime entendre le Grec et le rapporteur romain
Parler de ce peuple de Bretagne et dire l'innocence qu'il a dans le
    combat,
Et raconter sa joie et son amour de vivre;
J'aime leur entendre dire la couleur de ses yeux
Et qu'il offrait sa poitrine
Aux aigles des légions.

Auvergne que je verrai comme une roue de fonte, une giration soudain
    figée, un œil, un lac noirci par la chute des chênes, un soleil
Dont font pâture au centre les étourneaux, mais le chef couronné de
    pétales, passant ainsi l'hiver,
Sous les nuées, les coups que rien n'arrête depuis l'océan,
Dans les fils de la Vierge voyant naître son vrai fils,
Qui est l'astre même, et le cavalier de l'écume, et la soie rouge de notre
    chair.

Heureuse vallée! . . . A l'aube la troupe des poulains se rabat sous les
    pommiers,
Un homme monte,
Pour la première fois la terre est devant lui; les seigles sont bleus, ainsi
    que l'orge.

The west:
The Vendée softer than plumage,
The isles in the purple of rushes.

These are the spiritual lands, with their sad rain. The peatbog, the
    dripping muzzles,
A dog, a footbridge swayed by the wind,
Over there, between the hedgerows, where the fine rain is still
Beating down on a sound of carts and bells; on a fragrance of lime
    trees. . . . And the last star
Sways on its greasy stem.

Country! I kneel down, I touch the grass!
I count up your bones; I love your odor of wine and tobacco,
Of rough hairs and furs, of damp wings,
And the winter baggage trains in the gloom of the forests,
And the hunting horn, and the sea-conch, and the lighthouses turning.
I love to hear the Greek or the Roman recounting
Stories of Brittany's people, their innocence amidst battle,
Their joy, and their love of living;
And to hear of the color of their eyes
And how they offered their breast
To the legions' eagles.

Auvergne I'll see as a cast-iron wheel, a gyration abruptly congealed,
    an eye, a lake blackened by toppling oaks, a sun
At whose center the starlings pasture, but the head crowned with petals,
    thus passing the winter,
Under the stormclouds, the blows which nothing has stopped since the
    ocean,
Seeing its true son born in the gossamer's threads,
And the son is the star itself, and the horseman of foam, and the red silk
    of our flesh.

Fortunate valley! . . . At dawn the cluster of colts retreats to the apple
    trees,
A man goes up,
For the first time the earth lies before him; the ryefields are blue, and
    the barley.

Il sait lire l'écriture des coquelicots; il voit ce cœur affaîté, cette couronne de graphite dans les flammes,
Dans un brasier de nielle l'oiseau qui brûle, et le sphinx et le phénix sur le double fléau.
Il entre dans la demeure révélée: un duvet de feuillaison s'empare des chevaux de frise,
Venise s'exhausse des miroirs, partage comme une bogue son empire marin.
Dans l'incendie des ronciers, de son seul amour faisant sa robe d'armes,
De son lougre, sur la lame verte, offrant au vent toute la toile, salué, fêté par les corolles
Quand on lance sur la mer sa brassée de filets,
Dans un bruissement d'alouettes, —le cristal aspirant ses dernières couleurs, —
Voilà qu'il franchit la barre,
Et la Sainte sur son bûcher n'attendait plus que ce feu. Heureux amants qu'une même fortune lie,
A la limite de l'éternité
Brûlant et engendrant.

He can read the writing of poppies; he sees this heart tamed like a hawk, this crown of lead in the flames,
In the corncockles' brazier the bird all afire, and the phoenix and sphinx on the double scales.
He enters the dwelling revealed him: a soft spring down seizes the spiked defenses,
Venice rises from mirrors, shares her marine empire out like the husk of a chestnut.
In a bonfire of brambles, he makes his coat of mail of his only love,
In his fishing boat, on the green wave, offering all of his sail to the wind, saluted and fêted by petals
When his armful of nets is flung out on the sea,
In a rustling of larks—the crystal drawing in its last colors—
There, he's passed over the bar,
And the saint on her pyre was only awaiting this fire. Happy lovers linked by one fate,
At eternity's edge
Engendering and blazing.

CHARENTE

Alors on entend un bruit de pommes et de laiterie
Et la fumée par touffes noires s'amoncelle en haut.
Le dieu juste regagne la demeure souterraine
Dans une odeur de rouissage et de peausserie.

Les douze corbeaux qui régissent la balance,
Dans Lisbonne tiennent conseil sur la tombe du saint.
Que meure le grain, que pourrissent
Les fanes et les tiges des fèves; le taureau,

La chèvre et les autres bêtes qui parcourent le ciel
Ramassent derrière les nuées (comme nous autres les champignons
Ou les alises) provende d'étoiles brisées
Dont ils engraissent le soleil.

Vient l'oiseau où la fileuse fil à fil
Défait la trame de la mer.
Sur sa quenouille on le voit
Et sur le cristal bleu de la toiture.

Déjà la graisse des cochons flamboie
A travers la couenne tendue: doux soleil
Sur l'éponge noire des prés. Les enfants tournent la meule
Pour qu'on affûte les couteaux au manche de merisier.

Les remugles du calcaire et du bois
Atteignent la haute charpente des chapelles
Cachées dans des bocages de tilleuls.
Outres et vessies pendent aux battants,

L'avoine récoltée coule entre les voliges de châtaignier,
Le geai fracasse les dernières noix;
Sur le marais au goût de violettes pourries
Le chasseur écoute la sonnette du Saint-Sacrement.

~CHARENTE

Then a sound of apples, and of milking
And the smoke piles up in black tufts overhead.
The just god returns to his underground dwelling
In an odor of retting and dressing of hides.

The twelve crows that govern the scale
Hold council in Lisbon on the saint's tomb.
Let the seed die, and the fading leaves
And beanstalks rot; for the bull

The goat and the other beasts that wind through the sky
Are massing behind the clouds (as we might gather mushrooms
Or sorb-apples) the fodder of shattered stars
On which the sun grows fat.

The bird alights where the weaving woman, thread
By thread, is undoing the weft of the sea.
You will see it on her distaff
And on the blue crystal of the roof.

Already the pigs' fat flames
Through the stretched skins: soft sun on the black
Sponge of the marshland. The children are turning the grindstone
To whet the cherry-hafted knives.

Musty odors of limestone and wood
Rise to the high timberwork of the chapels
Concealed in the lime groves.
Wineskins and bladders dangle from the doors,   .

The fresh-mown oats stream out through the chestnut slats,
The bluejay shatters the last of the nuts;
On the marsh with its tang of violets rotting, the bell
Of the last Sacraments floats out to the hunter.

Ah! j'entends monter le chant grégorien
Et je ne vois pourtant que huttes de rouches,
Et la boue jaune de la Charente. Du noir et du bleu
Dont on a peint leurs planches

Les bateaux font avec les vaches des trous
Sur le versant oblique de la berge.
Vent de mer où l'oiseau lâche son cri et sa fiente!
Et puis ils chavirent dans la vase.

C'est nuit presque et un fanal d'eaux et de peupliers
Touche d'une lueur le martyre de l'apôtre Pierre
Qu'on a taillé dans la façade de l'église.
Derrière la grosse coquille Saint-Jacques qui sert de bénitier

Une femme range son balai. En pantoufles,
Elle s'en va entre les cyprès noirs.

Ah! I hear the plainsong rising
And yet I see only little rush huts,
And the yellow mud of the Charente. The blue and black
Of the painted boats

And the cows, make holes in the oblique
Slope of the bank.
Seawind, where the bird casts its cry and its droppings!
And then they capsize in the mire.

It's almost night, and a watchlight of water and poplars
Touches with a gleam the martyrdom of Peter
Carved in the church façade.
Behind the huge cockleshell of the stoup

A woman props her broom. In slippers,
She goes off between the black cypresses.

CHARENTE, ENCORE

Et c'est le phare blanchi de plumes, le haut fléau!
Un épandement sur les fascines pourries,
Le barbotement des jars, et les anguilles gaînées
Dont l'ouïe palpe l'herbe.

C'est un coq noir et bleu dans l'écharpe d'eau
Qui noue aux bêtes le bois triste.
C'est le meuglement doux des vaches
Sous les feuilles mouillées. . . Le clocher d'ocre

Et d'escargots monte au-dessus des marais:
Et c'est un lieu du monde, un centre parmi les choses.
Un feu de lampe, une flamme d'alambic
Bouge dans la voilure du matin.

Solitaire de l'automne, le cuivre se débat,
En esprit transmue les fruits de la terre, et l'alcool
Aux gants de gel traîne derrière l'hermine
Son faisceau de flèches acérées.

Les étourneaux basculent dans la vigne,
Toute pensée s'en va devant la prière;
De l'église romane je vois qu'il ne reste plus
Qu'un saint de pierre à gauche du vantail.

O fourrures mortes et froides qui faites tendre
La passion du chasseur; et sous ses doigts
Il sent durcir une larme de sang. . . Alors,
Par des gestes précis, il s'arrache à l'amour.

Il visite les espaliers, et les poires qui gonflent
Le rassurent. . . Il voit les greffes triompher,
Les bourgeons poindre et se fortifier; et dans les chais
Il écoute le mûrissement des liqueurs.

CHARENTE, AGAIN

And it's the plume-whitened lighthouse, the beam of the scale!
Strewn on bundles of rotting brushwood,
The ganders paddling about, and the sheathed eels
Whose gills are astir in the grass.

It is a cock, blue and black in the watery sash
Which loops the mournful woods to the herd.
It is cows lowing softly
Under dripping leaves. . . . A snailhorned and ochre

Steeple stands over the marshes:
And this is a place in the world, a center in things.
A lamp's flame, a flicker of pure distillation
Moves in the morning's sails.

And copper, the recluse of autumn, strives to transmute
The fruits of the earth into spirit. On the ermine's track
A bundle of whetted arrows
Trails from alcohol's frosty gloves.

The starlings rock up and down in the vine; all thought
Disappears in the presence of prayer;
Nothing's left of the Romanesque church but one stone
Saint on the left of the door.

O furs grown cold and dead, which can soften
The hunter's passion; and his fingertips feel
A tear of blood growing stiff. . . . After which,
With precise gestures, he wrenches himself free of love.

He visits his espaliered trees, and the swelling pears
Reassure him. . . . His grafts have succeeded;
His buds sprout and strengthen, and in his casks
He can hear the liquors maturing.

Graine noire, poudre et pays dans mes yeux,
D'eux, je fais mon four et je change en vérité
Ce qui n'est que chute, images tombées.

Black seed, homeland and powder blown in my eyes,
These make my furnace, where the Fall and windfallen
Images turn into truth.

⌒LOZERE

Ce pays de Lozère
Où les loups naguère
Troussaient les voyageuses,

Ce pays déchiré
De deux cris de coq,
Qu'une calèche traverse au galop,

Qu'un cheval affolé
Salit de bave et de gourme,
Ce pays qu'une corde rompt et crevasse

Ainsi qu'une peau,
Ce pays m'est une rose pétrifiée
Sur un rosier d'os.

Ce pays de voyage
S'acharne dans mon sang, me fait un rêve,
Me lie, me couche dans son lit de clous.

Ce pays rêve de moi,
Son silex m'entaille au front
Ou rouvre à mon genou ma blessure d'enfant.

Coq masqué, fille de plumes,
Charrette enrouée de bogues
Qu'un fou sanglant assassine,

Lozère aussi bien dirais-je Epidaure
Qu'un orage a calcinée,
Clytemnestre égorgée que les vautours aspirent.

Une mère maintenant vidée d'entrailles,
Quoi! qui suit son fils au calvaire
Dans les genévriers gris et le quartz.

⌒LOZERE

This land of Lozère
Where wolves lately lifted the skirts
Of lady travelers,

This land rent by two
Cockcrows, which a coach
Tears across at the gallop,

Stained by a maddened horse's
Mucus and lather, land
That a cord rifts and fissures

As if it were skin,
This land is my petrified rose,
On a rosetree of bone.

This voyage land seethes
In my blood, it raises a dream,
Binds me down on its litter of nails.

This land must have dreamt me, it notches
My brow with its flint, and reopens
The childhood cut on my knee.

Masked rooster, daughter of plumes,
Cart rusty with chestnut husks, slain
By a bloodstained buffoon,

Lozère, or as I might say
Epidaurus calcined by storms,
Clytemnestra, her throat slit, gasped in by vultures.

Now a mother empty of entrails,
But wait! She follows her son to the cross
Among the grey junipers and the quartz.

Lozère mon pays de voyages,
Mes os tout nus sous le soleil jetés,
Ma détresse, mon désir quêtés!

Là-bas perdre sa graisse moite. . .
Lozère tu n'as pas de fleurs:
Abattre le dernier oiseau

Et t'en faire un bouquet!

Voyage land, my Lozère,
My bones flung out bare in the sun,
My sought-after grief and desire!

There to lose one's moist flesh . . .
Lozère you have never known flowers:
There to kill the last bird

And make you a bouquet!

⌁DE MELUSINE

Nul guetteur casqué dans sa guérite de planches
N'a vu venir à travers le bocage de châtaigniers
La seule vierge plus sage que le serpent. O soleil

Que les oiseaux de mer épouillent dans un monceau de varech,
Veuf, tu caches sous les tombereaux tes oreilles de chien.
Vois les hommes manier la fourche, et leur tête rouge
Sous les chapeaux de cuir bouilli. N'aboie

Que si tout le château de Lusignan dort
Dans les fumées de vins et d'œillets.
Avec les sansonnets et les vignerons
Attends en Vendée qu'on remplisse les cuves.

Statues aux mains de sel! sur le plat pays
Vous levez vos armes. . . On vous voit la nuit
Sous des panaches. . . Les pommiers de leurs touffes
Frôlent le toit de verre. . . Tout mon sang,

Je le donne pour empourprer vos joues.
Oh! c'est déjà le vent d'été. . . Le bois
Des barques et des râteaux craque sous le bleu;
De toi, je n'ai trouvé que cette gaîne d'écailles
Qui ressemble à la pelure sèche d'une grosse couleuvre.

⌣MELUSINE

No helmeted lookout from his sentry box
Has seen the one virgin wiser than the serpent
Slip through the chestnut grove. O sun

That seabirds delouse in a heap of kelp,
Widower, hiding your dog's ears under the tumbrils.
Watch the men handling pitchforks, their heads bright red
Under their boiled leather hats. But don't bark

Unless the whole château of Lusignan
Falls asleep among wine fumes and pinks.
With the vineyard laborers and the starlings
Wait till the vats are filled in the Vendée.

Statues with hands made of salt! Your weapons rise
Over the flatlands. . . . You come with your nodding
Plumes in the night. . . . The apple trees' tendrils
Graze the glass roof. . . . All my blood,

I give just to redden your cheeks.
Already the summer wind. . . . The wooden
Rakes and ships' planks crack beneath the blue;
But of you I've found only this dry sheath of scales
Like the paring of some giant snake.

⁓METAMORPHOSE DES AMANTS

De partout la nuit craque et se fend
Et les amants se retrouvent couverts de plume
Avec un peu de sable sur les doigts.

Les amants ont soif dans leur lit desséché
Car toute l'eau est partie se noyer dans la mer;
Et les coqs à la fenêtre se poussent du jabot
Picorant dans la vitre les dernières étoiles.

Amants qui portez des panaches blancs et des couteaux
Saignez ces coqs et dans un plat de faïence
Répandez leur sang: qu'ils dorment, qu'ils dorment
Dans le cercle de craie où vos bras les ont clos.

⌁THE LOVERS' METAMORPHOSIS

Everywhere now the night shivers and cleaves
And the lovers find themselves covered in feathers
With a bit of fine sand on their fingers.

In their shrivelled bed the lovers thirst
For the water that's all gone to drown in the sea;
In the window the cocks jab about with their craws
And peck in the panes at the fading stars.

Lovers dressed in white feathers and knives
You must bleed these cocks and pour out their blood
In an earthenware bowl: let them sleep, in the chalk
Circle your arms close them in let them sleep.

⌢LES PIES

Les pies qui sont des anges blancs et noirs
Aiment les fourches, et le vent les chavire
Car elles sont trop lourdes de colliers d'yeux
Et de montres qu'elles écoutent dans l'eau.

Les pies couvent quand elles volent sur la crête du vent
Les œufs qu'elles ont volés aux carrières de gypse.

Laissant toute nue la mariée,
Dans l'arbre funéraire elles comptent son trousseau
Et tressent pour son front leurs couronnes d'épines.

Pies qui picorez l'éternelle doublure du vent
Sur ce bûcher d'écaille il faut périr
Où les poissons viennent pour la mue.

⌣THE MAGPIES

The magpies, angels in black and white,
Love tree forks, and the wind will capsize them
For they're much too heavy with their necklaces of eyes
And watches they listen to under the water.

As they ride the wind's furl the magpies brood
On the eggs they stole from the gypsum quarries.

Leaving the bride stripped bare, they count up
Her trousseau on the funeral tree
And plait their crowns of thorns for her brow.

Magpies who peck at the wind's eternal folding
You will perish here on this pyre of scales
Where the fish venture in for the moulting.

TAUREAUX DANS BAYONNE

Nous voici dans la cuve et sur les planches liés;
Un soleil d'arachide et de crin reste entre les toitures;
Ocre soir que les pigeons becquètent! on voit la face énorme des marchands de bestiaux, et leur ventre barré de chaînes d'or.
Les diacres en rabats blancs hantent des hauts lieux de meulière où la giration des moulins ressemble aux volées d'anges. Lauriers et magnolias absorbent les tennis, et des charrois d'hirondelles
Coulent dans le bleu mouillé.

Nuit, que des chevaux conduisent en tournant,
Vous descendez comme la vis au centre d'un pressoir
Et sans doute du sang se mêle au moût de la vendange.
Comme des oiseleurs à cheval sur la frontière épient le passage des migrations,
Je vous vois en costume de lumière à la pliure des deux mondes.
Tout un peuple vous croit grimés quand seuls vous êtes nus;
Dans un ciel de combat, de sa peau de fauve vêtue, poudrée de pluies de météores, la nuit aux blanches cornes
Charge et mugit en bavant de l'écume.
Lui, tout silencieux dans le sable, par danses et véroniques, trace la ligne sacrée
Où mortellement l'estoc coupe le pivot. . . O pervenches, alors vous versez vos flots de bleu.
Avec le flux, les oranges déferlent; les forêts se déploient et gagnent les champs de courses.
Bleus sont les chariots, et les chiens solitaires lèchent la sciure rose des boucheries;
Un vent s'élève qui plaque en haut les fumées des crématoires;
Du Guadalquivir monte un bruit de grelots; ou bien c'est dans l'Adour un sifflement de scories. Couvertes de loques et de dartres, les haridelles trébuchent sur les rails, et on sent
Derrière les rideaux métalliques
L'odeur fade des nègres et des bananes.
O vous, au visage de mortels, qui dansez dans l'entre-deux des mondes,
Vous êtes dans l'arbre attachés par la nuque,
Aussi vos pieds dans le sable marquent peu.

⌢BULLS IN BAYONNE

Here we are in the wine-vat, and bound on the boards;
The sun like a nut-colored mane between the rooftops;
And pigeons peck at the ochre evening. The cattle dealers' huge faces
    appear, and their paunches barred with gold chains.
Deacons trailing white bands haunt the millstone heights, where the
    windmills revolve like soaring angels. The tennis courts vanish into
    magnolia and laurel, and convoys of swallows
Glide through the moistened blue.

Night driven by turning horses,
Wound down like the central screw of a press
And blood no doubt sharpens the must of the vintage.
As on the frontier fowlers on horseback spy the passing migrations,
I see you costumed in light where the two worlds fold under.
A whole people sees you in greasepaint when you are the only nudes;
In a heaven of combat, dressed in his pelt and powdered with meteor
    showers, the white-horned night
Charges and bellows with foaming muzzle.
He, in utter silence upon the sand, with dances and veronicas, traces the
    sacred line
Where the sword's point mortally severs the pivot. . . . Then the peri-
    winkles' blue tides pour out.
With the flux, the orange tree breaks into foam; the forests unfurl on the
    racetracks.
Blue are the carts, and solitary dogs lap up the rosy sawdust of butcher
    shops;
A wind rises to fan out the crematory smoke on high;
From the Guadalquivir comes a sound of sheep bells, or else it's the
    hissing of slag in the Adour. Covered with rags and scurf, the old
    horses totter along the rails, and we smell
Behind the metallic curtains
The stale scent of bananas and Negroes.
O you, with your mortal faces, who dance in the interspace of the
    worlds,
You're attached to the tree by your napes,
So your feet barely leave a mark in the sand.

Vous ressemblez aux pendus qui s'allongent en sursauts: (la bouche
veut de l'air, les pieds un point d'appui...)
Vous ressemblez aux dormeurs qu'un rêve ou bien l'alcool mettent
verticaux... Ils chancellent
Mais voyagent immobiles dans cet étrange froid
Que les ailes des pigeons laissent sur les joues.
Vêtus de raide chasuble,
Et la cornée de l'œil d'un blanc de gouache,
Pieds joints, vous avancez sur la houle des sismogrammes. Aux limites
de l'Eden, vous relevez de leur garde les anges: Perséphone fuit et
la femme de Minos invoque la fleur blanche du narcisse.
En vos mains tous pouvoirs sont remis: vous liez et vous déliez les
grâces et les forces;
A vos gestes soumises, les eaux descendent et foudroient... Vous
saluez!... Les mules traînent le taureau, mais la mort est si belle
qu'il la suit sur l'échelle de soie.
Dans l'écume amère des goémons le vaisseau creuse sa gîte; d'aucun
secours nous sont les feux; on dirait
Que naître est notre lot à ce monde sans repère.
Reine crétoise, cette cuirasse vous sied, faite de la graisse des oies. Dans
le berceau de ses cornes, votre coude est posé
Et la brise en aigrette ébouriffe à son front
De blanches boucles... Comme peints à la fresque, immobiles en vos
demeures,
Vous régnez sur un ciel de jonquilles et de pommes;
Mais du solstice votre chute s'aggrave. Sous sa custode de crustacé, il
descend et tue
L'ange d'en haut! Aux chiennes des marais, il lance les loques.
Fouillant sables et limons, vous rassemblez le corps,
Vous arrachez aux mâchoires des épaves de chair;
Par souffles et salive, vous bâtissez! Il voit.
Il entend battre les ailes de l'oiseau.
Haute proue rougie à des feux de forgeron,
Coule dans l'ouest la longue barque.
O moi de forges en moissons, et dans l'effroi de plates eaux,
Là où tremblent des reflets!
Ou bien je suis sous la cascade des bétonnières, au plein vent des chan-
tiers métalliques,
Dans le gel estival et brûlant des grandes herses de montagne.

Like hanged men who start and stretch out: (the mouth seeking air, the
   feet a fulcrum. . . .)
Like sleepers fetched upright by alcohol or by dreams. . . . They waver
But travel immobile in the strange cold
The pigeons' wings leave on their cheeks.
Dressed in rigid vestments,
The cornea white as gouache,
Feet joined, you advance on the seismograms' swell. At the limits of
   Eden, you relieve the angelic guard: Persephone flees, and the bride
   of Minos invokes the white flower of the narcissus.
All powers are placed in your hands: you bind and unbind the graces
   and forces;
Subject to your gestures, the waters cascade and thunder. . . . You bow!
   . . . The mules drag off the bull, but death is so lovely he follows it
   up the silk ladder.
In the bitter spume of the seaweed the ship heels still deeper; no beacon
   can help us;
You'd say it's our lot to be born in this world without landmarks.
Cretan queen, this breastplate becomes you, made out of goosefat. In
   the cradle of his horns, you pose your elbow,
And the breeze ruffles up the white curls on his brow
Like a plume. . . . Like paintings in fresco, immobile deep in your
   dwellings,
You reign in a sky of apples and jonquils; and yet
Since the solstice your fall has grown swifter. Behind his encrusted pyx-
   cloth, the angel from on high
Leans down and makes the kill! He flings out the tatters to marsh dogs.
Scouring through silt and sand, you reassemble the body,
Stripping the derelict flesh from the jawbones;
You build with your breath and saliva! And he sees.
He hears the bird's wings beating.
Its prow still red from the blacksmith's flames,
The long ship goes down in the west.
There I am in the forge come to harvest, in dread of dead waters, among
The trembling reflections!
Or else beneath the cement mixer's flow, in the high wind of the metal
   gantries,
In the scorching summer frost of the great mountain harrows.

Ou bien me référant à des cartes de cosmographie
Je compte vos pas dans l'envers. . . J'épie le trouble qui peut naître
      quand il vous portera dans la laitance marine; ô Grèce célestielle,
      verrai-je à vos rivages toucher le couple,
En haut le lys
Porter l'unique rédempteur?

De rames et de clous je fais mon autre demeure; vous froissez dans le
      port des lunes de pétrole,
Pluies qui tenez droites sur les rampes du laurier.
De violettes mâchées je colmate mon vaisseau,
Les dernières galernes nous inclinent le cœur:
Bayonne! Bayonne des Basques,
Les amarres rompues nous coupons la frontière des eaux;
Devant nous la mer ruminante au goût de nacre et d'œillet:
Un vent de paille déjà sèche nos lessives,
Le suroît se colore du bois rouge des forêts.
Mais le bois qu'a rougi le sang du crucifié,
Le bois vertical qui teint nos sacrements,
Le bois où Jésus répandit la teinture du sang,
Le mât!
C'est nous qui le portons.

Or else, consulting cosmographical maps,
I follow your steps through the other side. . . . I glimpse the stress to be
  born when he carries you off in the sea-milt; will I ever see the
  couple touching your shores, celestial Greece,
The lily bearing on high
The only redeemer?

With nails and oars I make my other dwelling; the rains that stand
  straight on the laurel slopes
Ruffle the gasoline moons in the harbor.
I seal my ship with the violets' pulp,
Our hearts veer beneath the last northwest winds:
Bayonne! Bayonne of the Basques,
Breaking our moorings we cross the waters' frontier;
Before us the ruminant sea, with its tang of pinks and mother-of-pearl:
Already a wind of straw has dried out our washing,
The sou'wester takes on the deep red of the forests.
But the wood which the Crucifixion reddened,
The vertical wood which tinges our sacraments,
Where Jesus poured out the tincture of blood,
The mast!
It is ourselves who bear it.

II

FROM
Travaux sur la terre
(1966)

⌐*FROM* TRAVAUX POUR UN BUCHER

Vous n'avez plus que ce bleu de lune des blanchisseries,
Cette flamme sur les figuiers que fait le linge des bûcherons.
Secret tourment des tournesols, corps sanctifié,
Il s'engouffre dans les vapeurs.

Beau bêlement d'agneau (toujours sur un lit de cendre
On canonise les saints), pelote d'échardes, rouelle de chardon,
Me guident vers Delphes à tâtons.

Volez-nous ce monde, marquez-nous d'étoiles,
Emmenez les filles faner, qu'elles enfantent dans l'herbe,
Ou qu'elles pondent des œufs sous le laurier.

Que je descende comme un pédoncule, que je me déroule comme la
        crosse d'une fougère;
Qu'elle soit fumée rose de saumon, rosée d'alchimiste,
Au bout de mes nerfs (déjà!) paillettes blanches de gel!
Qu'il me soit un poignard à travers le cœur celui dont le soleil entendit
        craquer les vertèbres,
Là-bas, au centre du Pacifique. Il arrive que le rosier porte un seul
        bouton,
Et la chenille l'étrangle. Flux, reflux d'équinoxe, malgré tout.
Respiration, dilatation. Ici, des fleuves;
Là, le cavalier se dessèche et devient une longe de cuir.
Bucrânes, blancs fémurs aux têtes de massue, voilà ce qui reste quand
        il a passé
Sa langue sur le troupeau. Ils m'ont meurtri,
Et je ne suis plus que cette pierre creuse où fleurit le sureau.

Au moins entendrai-je l'alouette essorer des luzernes, la chute et le
        cahotement d'un chariot. La nuit parfois s'emplit de bourrache.
        Avec une poignée d'orties la gardeuse d'oies récure le chaudron.
Plumes, lunules de hiboux gonflent les ténèbres. Le dernier coquelicot,
        le dernier cor de chasse trouent l'ovale du miroir
Où le cerisier se renverse.

⌒FROM WORK FOR A PYRE

Now you have only this moon-blue of the laundries,
This flame on the fig trees made by the loggers' wash.
The secret torment of sunflowers, sanctified body,
Is engulfed in the mists.

The bleating of lambs (it's always on cinder-beds
The saints are canonized), ball of prickles and starry thistle
Guide me tapping to Delphi.

Steal this world from us, stamp us with stars,
Bring the girls to the hay-making, let them give birth in the grass,
Or lay eggs beneath the laurel.

Let me descend like a stalk, unroll like the croziered fern;
Let her be a smoky salmon pink, the alchemist's dew,
At the end of my nerves (already!) white spangles of frost.
Let him be a dagger through my heart, whose vertebrae the sun heard
    crack,
There in the Pacific's center. The rose-tree comes to bear a single bud
Which the caterpillar strangles. Ebb, flow of the equinox, in spite of it
    all.
Respiration, dilation. Here, rivers;
There, the horseman dries out to a leather rein.
Ox-skulls, white bludgeon-headed femurs, that's what's left when he
    has passed
His tongue across the herd. They've battered me,
And now I am only this hollow stone where the blackberry flowers.

At least I'll hear the lark soar from the alfalfa, the fall and jolting of a
    hayrick. Sometimes the night fills up with borage. With a fistful of
    nettles the goosegirl scours the cauldron.
Feathers, moonlets of owls swell the shadows. The last poppy, the last
    hunting horn, tunnel the mirror's oval
Where the cherry tree is transposed.

C'est mon pays, c'est mon domaine:
Les buses miaulent dans l'éther,
L'épicéa respire un éternel été; dans l'allée de cyprès les statues me
    regardent,
Nymphes dont les yeux aujourd'hui ne sont plus que guêpiers, —meute
    grecque figée dans les ronces écarlates
Qui saigne pourtant du sang de mon vrai dieu.
Un fagot de seringa flambe au milieu de la plaine où les journaliers
    chargent les charrettes.
Parfois l'un d'eux s'appuie de l'aisselle sur le manche de sa fourche
Et le tabac qu'il a roulé fume bleu, et la boucle blanche de la fumée
    s'en va.
Quel clou me tue que le muet langage du peuplier même enfonce!
Vainement le vainqueur retire de sa chair le harpon,
Il sait. Et combien l'autre qui n'est plus qu'un soir de bal,
Une cocarde foulée. Heureux l'ami mort
Pour qui les chevaux vont hennir. Heureux le poisson
Qui brille encore au moment de mourir.
Clé! mais comme en met au joug le bouvier
Pour mieux serrer de cordes et lanières le front des bêtes.
Derrière les buis poudrés de pluie d'orage, j'entends les grands aruspices
Qui ont faim de viande. Un instant ils s'attardent au milieu du chemin
    pour suivre des yeux les limaces rouges,
Qu'ils sectionnent d'un sifflement de baguette, et il gicle une gelée
    pareille à un œil crevé,
Tandis que les enfants avec leurs palmes chassent les mouches.
Un bruit d'ébranchage à coups de serpe nous vient
A cause du vent qui porte à plein sur les régions boisées;
Les forêts de Pharaon, Brocéliande, et celle où les feuilles prophétisent,
On les fauche, on amoncelle les troncs, on lie, accumule les fagots.
    De dédale en dédale
Les gerbiers lèvent dans les cours leur cloche jaune
D'où les cyclistes voient de loin les hirondelles s'échapper.
Moins loin, un épouvantail à chapeau de feutre défend le champ de
    fèves. Le bouc pue,
Le geai jacasse et le linge ne bouge plus
Ni sur le fil ni sur le figuier.

It's my country, it's my domain:
The buzzards mew in the ether,
The spruce breathes an eternal summer; in the cypress alley the statues
    stare at me,
Nymphs whose eyes today are but wasps' nests—Greek pack clotted in
    the scarlet brambles
Which bleeds, however, the blood of my true god.
A bundle of vines flames in the plain where the journeymen load the
    carts.
Sometimes one of them rests his armpit on the pitchfork's handle
And his rolled tobacco smokes blue, and the white curl goes off.
What nail is killing me, that even the poplar's mute language drives
    deeper!
In vain the victor draws the harpoon from his flesh,
He knows. And the other still more, who now is only the hour after the
    ball,
A trampled rosette. Happy the dead friend
For whom the horses will whinny. Happy the fish
Still shining at the moment of death.
Key! but as the drover locks the yoke
The better to fasten with thongs and cords the brows of the oxen.
Behind the boxwood powdered with storm rain, I hear the great diviners
Hungry for meat. They linger a moment on the road to watch the red
    slugs,
Which they slice with a whistling of wands, spurting a squashed eye-
    jelly,
While the children with their palm-leaves chase the flies.
We can hear a faint lopping of branches
Because the wind stands strongly from the wooded regions;
The forests of Pharaoh, and Broceliande, and the wood of prophetic
    leaves,
Are leveled, the trunks are in piles, the bundles tied and gathered. From
    labyrinth to labyrinth
The corn-ricks in barnyards raise their yellow bells
From which, at a distance, cyclists see swallows escaping.
Nearer, a felt-hatted scarecrow defends the beanfield. The he-goat stinks,
The jay jabbers and the laundry moves
No longer on the line or on the fig tree.

O vous qui avez des bracelets de cuir lacés aux poignets,
Leveurs de gerbes, porteurs de traverses, Argiens aux armes emmanchées de cornouiller,
Dans vos toisons caille la saumure des mers
Et quand vous revenez les veaux s'approchent des clôtures pour vous lécher.
Grands mâles privés de femmes qui tombez la nuit sur le lin,
Brisés par les grands travaux, ceints de silence et de fatigue,
Dans le sommeil encore un morceau de jour vous reste entre les paupières,
Esquille où l'aube prend son linge, et puis la torsion de vos muscles vous réveille
Quand elle a fui déjà, mouillant le ciel à peine d'un peu de poudre de papillon.
J'entends la conque qui rassemble les sardiniers: les feux s'allument sur la plage et les murailles troyennes noircissent.
Une fois de plus la terre est toute seule dans l'espace.
Les plongeurs l'ont abandonnée en emportant les fleurs de nénuphars.

Les dieux qui ne savent compter que jusqu'à neuf
Escaladent la perche et la tête sous l'aile
Dorment. Ils ont tiré l'échelle. Ils couvent l'œuf
Sur le toit que convoite le serpent
Couveur lui aussi en célestes couvaisons.
Les rois et les charrons qui enduisent de graisse
Le moyeu des chars en haut jusqu'à neuf
Voient les dieux sur leurs doigts compter le même compte
Deux chevaux au timon et le cheval de flèche
Trois chars l'aurige qui conduit le dieu caché
L'autre le troisième emporte les javelots
Avec leurs ailes de criquets rouges et jaunes
Les Hellènes vont au-dessus des champs de mil
Guêpières partout antennes épis fauchés.

. . . .

Le busard tient tout seul sur ses plumes,
En haut du feu, et tout seul gémit dans la solitude
Qu'enneige l'œil aveuglé par la poussière des fenaisons.

You whose wrists are laced with leather bracelets,
Sheaf-pitchers, men carrying ties, Argives with ash-handled spears,
The brine clots in your fleeces
And when you return the calves come up to the fences to lick you.
Great males without women who fall at night on the linen,
Worn by great works, wrapped in fatigue and silence,
In sleep one fragment of daylight is left between your eyelids,
A splinter where dawn snags her laundry, and then your stretching
     muscles awake you
When she has already fled, just moistening the sky with a bit of butterfly
     powder.
I hear the conch that gathers the sardine boats, the fires are lit on the
     shore and the Trojan walls blacken.
Once more the earth is all alone in space.
The divers abandoned her, carrying off the water lilies.

The gods, who can only count up to nine
Climb to their perches and, head under wing,
Sleep. They've pulled up the ladder. They're brooding on the egg
On the roof, that the serpent covets
Brooder himself on heavenly nests.
The kings and wheelwrights on high who rub
The chariot hubs with grease see the gods counting
To nine on their fingers, counting the same count
Two horses on the shaft, and the leader
Three chariots, the charioteer who drives, the hidden god
The other, the third, carries off the javelins
With their red and yellow locust wings
The Hellenes pass above the millet fields
Everywhere wasp-waists, antennas, leveled blades.

. . . .

The buzzard on his feathers hangs alone,
Above the fire, and cries alone in the solitude
Made snowy by an eye blinded with the dust of hay-making.

Il gémit, il miaule, hostile aux crémations;
En flèche s'aiguise, se transperce, tombe,
Rebondit et se cloue au zéro de la cible.
Vivants et morts disparaissent, guerre et meurtre s'effacent,
Cône et sphère composent le champ troyen
Où la céruse nivelle les moissons. Une coque noire
Sur le sable, une coquille pilée dans la pâte,
Une crinière que le flux repousse.
Du bout de l'aile il touche la peau tendue
Et la vibration s'inscrit à la surface de l'eau,
Lève les libellules et les moissonneurs
Qui rejoignent leurs machines aériennes.
Pour incendier le repaire ils feront de paille
Leur cheval de Troie et de leur dard ouvriront
Les volets humides des chambrières.
Ah, Astarté,
Que le jasmin gagne ta chair insolente!
Ah, ce corps maculé de digitales
Qui empourpre la verrière!
Déjà Byzance nous maquille,
Éteint la torche, empierre le bûcher,
Nous montre le tombeau la plus sûre galère;
Tandis que les mules qui ont tiré
Jusqu'ici les troncs urinent dans la poussière,
Tandis qu'à cheval on se dispute l'or,
Tandis que les marchands débattent du cubage
Et que les bûcherons crachent le vin rouge;
Tandis que perle la résine aux blessures de l'aubier
Et que nous autres de nos capes nous chassons les buses
Qui font un dais sur le bûcher.

Les dieux sont immortels mais ils vivent masqués
Qu'ils changent de visage et nous croyons changée
Leur nature pourtant qui est surnaturelle
Puisqu'en Un ils sont trois et multiples de trois
Peuplent l'Olympe et le Nil les îles les bois.

Il reste que l'été sur un trépied de bois
N'est plus que la boule bleue que les laveuses ont laissée.

He cries, mews, hostile to cremations;
Sharpens to an arrow, pierces himself and falls,
Rebounds, and nails himself against the bull's eye.
Living and dead disappear, murder and war are effaced,
Cone and sphere compose the Trojan field
Where dead-white flattens the harvests. A black hull
On the sand, a shell ground into the paste,
A mane which the floodtide pushes back.
With his wingtip he touches the stretched skin
And the vibration signs itself on the water's surface,
Lifts the dragonflies and harvesters
Who join their aerial machines.
To set the lair aflame they'll make
Their Trojan horse of straw, and with their darts
Open the humid blinds of roommaids.
Ah, Astarte,
May jasmine pervade your insolent flesh!
Ah, this body, maculate with foxglove
Whose purple stained the glass windows!
Already Byzantium makes up our face,
Puts out the torch, turns the pyre to stone,
Shows us the tomb is the surest galley;
While the mules that pulled
The trunks here urinate in the dust,
While on horseback the gold is disputed,
While the merchants argue the cordage
And the loggers spit red wine;
While resin pearls on the gashes in the sapwood
And with our capes we chase the buzzards
That canopy the pyre.

The gods are immortal but they live in masks
When they change faces we believe their nature
Changed which yet is supernatural
Since in One they are three, and multiples of three
They people Olympus and the Nile the isles the woods.

At last the summer on a wooden tripod
Is only the blue ball left by the washerwomen.

A coups de battoir elles écrasent le linge
Et la mousse qui monte éclabousse leur chair
Dont les amants trop loin cueillent la blanche lèpre.
Prunes dans le verger que les frelons saccagent:
Deux lèvres, une plaie où coule un sucre amer,
Les chaumes en biseau qui transpercent la pulpe;
Des rides, des taches, des trous que les fourmis taraudent,
Des menstrues qui mettent à nu le noyau;
Les facettes des yeux, les poils, les brosses,
Tout travaille à tout détruire, immonde mère
Qui se farde la nuit pour être plus féconde
Et dévore en plein jour les fruits de la rosée.
Patrocle seul sur le catafalque des fûts
Quand tout est chute aspire au feu. Les saintes flammes
Qui lavent jusqu'à l'or la matière laissée aux fentes des montagnes,
Celles mêmes qui sont la paille où nichent les salamandres,
Celles qu'aucun vent ne renverse et pourtant que la Pentecôte retourne,
Celles qui survivent au bois, foulent l'anneau pythique du serpent,
Celles-là mêmes qui vêtent de bleu les madones en plâtre,
Celles qui sont du ciel l'ombilic et qu'on voit dans le miroir des dieux,
Celles-là mêmes consument le bûcher
Où Troie déjà se transfigure.

They beat the laundry with the washing-club
And the rising lather splashes their flesh
Whose leprous whiteness distant lovers gather.
Plums in the orchard sacked by hornets:
Two lips, a wound where sour sugar flows,
The beveled straws transfixing the pulp;
Wrinkles, stains, holes threaded by ants,
Menstrual ooze baring the pit within;
Faceted eyes, the hairs, the brushy legs,
All works to destroy all, foul mother
Who paints herself at night to become more fertile,
Devouring by daylight the fruits of the dew.
Patrocles alone on the catafalque of logs
When all is falling aspires to the flame. The holy flames
Which rinse to gold the matter of mountain clefts,
Which are themselves the straw where salamanders nest,
Which no wind reverses but the Pentecost bends back,
Which survive the wood, thrust down the serpent's Pythian ring,
The same which clothe in blue the plaster madonnas,
Which are the sky's navel and which are seen in the mirror of the gods,
The same which consume the pyre
Where already Troy is transfigured.

⌒ZURBARAN

Cette étoile de pain des bergers fut l'hostie
Ce lait de chaux rigide où blanchissent les saintes
Et le linge trempé de calcaire m'habille
D'un même feu cuisant la coquille et le pain

J'aime dans ce désert la dure résidence
Dans la pierre le feu dont les feuilles sont blanches
Cette aube ce printemps cette argile et ce gel
Et la pelle et le four dont use le mitron

Que le même astre blanc s'imprime dans la houille
Ou que l'eau dans la nuit le prenne et le renvoie
On voit que ces miroirs dans l'âme pétrifient

Ce que cherche le temps à corrompre à détruire
Les Apôtres le Christ sur l'aire méditant
En robe d'amiante habillent leur église

⌒ZURBARAN

This starlike bread was the shepherds' host
This rigid whitewash where the saints grow pale
I am dressed in the linen steeped in limestone
Whose flame bakes the cockleshell and the bread

I love in this desert its harsh residence
The flame whose leaves have gone white in the stone
This dawn this spring this frost and this clay
And the baker's boy with his oven and scoop

Whether the same white star prints the coal
Or whether night's waters take it, return it
We see that the soul's mirrors petrify

That which time would corrupt and destroy
Meditating on threshing floors, the Apostles and Christ
Clothe their church in asbestos robes

POUR LE DOUZIEME ANNIVERSAIRE
DE LA MORT DE MANOLETE

Et seulement pleurez le mortel dont Méduse
Evite la rencontre; à l'autre le désert
Est un jardin, le fruit du mal n'est pas offert,
La grâce seulement comme parfaite ruse.

Car la grâce est ici le leurre dont on use;
La mort s'y dompte à coups de foudre, à rien ne sert
Le défi quand il faut la vaincre sans les nerfs,
Pour l'autre l'incarner qui d'abord la refuse.

La Mère goûte en haut à la précoce écume
D'une vendange d'août, en bas on le parfume
Effeuillant sur ses yeux le nard et le jasmin.

O Cordoue, il sied aux géraniums ce matin
D'encombrer tout le ciel: plus d'aube, plus de fête
Où ne croisse en soleil l'ombre de Manolete.

FOR THE TWELFTH ANNIVERSARY
OF THE DEATH OF MANOLETE

Mourn only the mortal whom even Medusa
Fears to encounter; as for the other, for him
The desert's a garden, no apple of evil is offered,
And grace only comes as a perfect ruse.

For grace here is the red lure they use;
Death is tamed by lightnings. No point in a challenge
When it must be overcome without nerves, and the other
Incarnate all that he first refused.

Above, the Mother savors the early froth
Of an August vintage, below they let fall
Petals of spikenard and jasmine on his eyes.

O Cordova, your geraniums should overrun
The skies this morning: no more feasts, and no dawn
Save where Manolete's shade grows higher with the sun.

VERONIQUE

Ce juillet de chiffon rouge n'a pas fini
De boucher ma mémoire, et seul était fleuri
Le laurier; plus d'oiseaux, rien que paille; l'écume
M'incisait les yeux; un astre, un phare s'allume.

Lugubre bête, un monde a gîté pour la nuit,
Tassé, la dent longue; un monde, un énorme fruit
D'échardes, bogue, noix, herse ou serpent à plumes
De fer, silencieux comme un centre d'enclume.

Il y eut cette crête en haut des lys de mer
Et dans l'esprit de sel ce voyage de noces,
Des transhumances, des élus au sacerdoce

Ouvrant d'immenses fleurs, parcourant des déserts.
Il y eut ce visage essuyé, ce visage
Imprimé dans l'étoffe—en vrai, en témoignage.

VERONICA

This July of red cloth unceasingly cuts off
My memory, only the laurel had bloomed;
No more birds, only straw; the lather etched
At my eyes; a lighthouse, a star is alight.

Sad beast, a world is bedded down tonight,
Hunched over and famished; a world, an enormous fruit
Of burrs, husks, prickles, a harrow or iron-plumed
Serpent; and still, as the anvil's still center.

Above the sea-lilies this crest appeared
And in the spirit of salt this honeymoon voyage,
Upward driftings of Alpine flocks, the divine

Elect spreading huge flowers, crossing the deserts.
This face appeared, wiped dry, this face
Impressed in the cloth—in truth, and as a sign.

BANDERILLES NOIRES

Quelle bête de suif et salive a mouillé
Mes os que me voilà tout de nocturnes linges
Tatoué? Dans mon dos qui navigue? Je feins,
Je décide l'oubli. Son mufle m'a fouillé

Les épaules, un lys maintenant me marque, un
Gel précoce qui déploie au-dessus de mes reins
Je sais quelle toile où la coutume a taillé
Son manteau de limon, un drap où le noyé

Dégorge son eau, un lambeau de brumes, un
Jeu de flèches (fuseaux noirs qu'on m'aurait plantés
Pour descendre aux Enfers!) Tout cri qui monte en vain,

Fumée, image, peu de sang pour ces vérités
Qui lèchent des parois d'astres morts, et sans fin
Raclent dans le cuveau l'amertume du vin.

BLACK BANDERILLAS

What beast of saliva and suet has moistened my bones
That I am tattooed all over with this
Nocturnal linen? Who's sailing my back? I dissemble,
Decide on oblivion. His muzzle has rummaged

My shoulders, I'm marked with a lily now, an early
Frost unfurls across my loins the remembered
Cloth from which custom has cut
Its cloak of silt, its sheet where the drowned man

Coughs up his water, a tatter of haze,
An archery (black spindles planted in me for
The descent to the Underworld)! Every cry that goes up

In vain, smoke or image, little blood for these
Truths that lick the shells of dead stars, and forever
Scrape up in the vat the wine's bitter lees.

FAENA DE CAPA

Qu'une aile, qu'un pétale, apaisent tant de force,
Qu'une étoffe éployée amène dans ses plis
Ces muscles en paquets qui tendent leurs poignards,
Que l'œil et que l'esprit gouvernent ce chaos,

Qu'à l'orange, à la rose obéisse la nuit,
Qu'à la flamme qu'on feint s'embrase le charbon,
Que le sang, dans un feu, dans un bruit d'éventail
Se rallume, s'éteigne et bouillonne et se noie,

Que le monde soit vu dans un cercle de planches:
Ses grèves, ses voiliers (astres majeurs, planètes),
Sa chute, son duel que la grâce résout;

Que soit la cinquième heure heure d'éternité,
Que l'on soit n'importe où et qu'on soit au milieu
Fait le cœur en ce lieu terrain de vérité.

⌒FAENA DE CAPA

Let a petal, a wing, subdue all this might,
Let a spreading cloth draw deep in its folds
These clustered muscles extending their blades,
Let the eye and the spirit govern this chaos,

Let the orange, the rose, be obeyed by the night,
And the dead coals light up at this seeming blaze,
And the blood, in a fire, in a soft sound of fans
Rekindle and die, boil over and drown,

Let the world be seen in a circle of boards:
Its shores and ships sailing (planets, major stars),
Its fall, and its duel which grace accords;

Let the hour of eternity now be the fifth,
Let us be anywhere, and be at the core—
Makes the heart here the terrain of the truth.

SALAMANDRE

Salamandre, ce nid d'écumes et de joncs,
Ce Parnasse de poudre où la hache tournoie,
C'est comme dans Paros: quand la muse se noie
Il faut que les dauphins la tirent des filons.

Il faut dans les filets trouver le loup de soie
Qui tombe avec la nuit; il faut courir au long
Des grèves, prévenir par cris, à coups de gong
Que sel est la statue où l'aube se déploie.

Rincez ce trou, massacrez ces pigeons, tendez
Sur le bois d'olivier la flanelle écarlate,
Que le pourrissement des mouches qui éclatent

(En quels lointains secrets maintenant dégradés)
Serve à notre salut. De votre chair d'abeilles,
O Vierge, j'ai dit les guérisons, les merveilles.

⌒SALAMANDER

Salamander, this nest of rushes and foam,
This powder Parnassus and whirling axe,
Remind me of Paros: the dolphins must drag
The drowning muse from the buried lodes.

We must take the black silken mask in our nets
When it falls with the night; we must cry, run down
The beaches, give warning with blows of our gong
That salt is the statue unfurling the dawn.

Kill these pigeons, rinse out this fissure, and spread
Scarlet flannel out on the olive wood,
That the blaze and bursting of rotting flies

(Now sunk to what secret depths) may serve
Our salvation. And now, great Virgin, I've named
Your bees' flesh, and told of its marvels and cures.

ODE NUMERO 8

La voilure a brûlé,
Et je suis là où les mondes plient, à la merci des chiens, dieu devenu en
    quelque sorte, épaulant la voûte
Où les missiles cognent parfois contre un morceau de toiture,
Un palais de Rome emporté, un cheveu d'Ophélie.
Ceux qui frayent dans la nuit, ceux qui germent sur une fiente d'astres,
Après coassent à l'abri des bardanes et des tambours de guerre.
Ce braiement, vous l'entendez sur la route d'Egypte;
Et le souffle des coureurs de fond, je l'aspire encore
A la bouche des grottes infernales.
Ici l'empereur des trois mondes me convie à boire cette buée où l'éternel
    féminin en perle coagule.
L'eau des antres, la conque striée, l'arc
Où Diane nue ajuste son corps—et je la vois après sortie d'un bain de
    Hollande,
Vêtue de jute   L'eau revient sur le marais,
Il fait une éternité au lobe transparent.

L'âne aussi fut une ruche où l'armoise nourrissait les abeilles.

La porte s'ouvre et l'hymen est surpris dans la baille de bois où le savon
    écume.
Le corbeau disperse sur les prés le linge de la passion: "Ah, soleil, dis-je,
    séchez ce pain
En forme de croissant pour Diane chasseresse qui retourne à son bain."
J'en étais au vert émeraude à cause de la mer qui m'avait longtemps
    nourri,
Les bûches goudronnées sous les pattes des mouettes n'avaient plus la
    blonde humeur dont s'enivrent les bûcherons.
A suivre sur la feuille l'escargot je comptais une à une les spires, en
    même temps combien de courbes il fallut pour caréner la nef Argo.
La part de Dieu qui gouverne les nombres impairs ajoutée au chiffre de
    l'homme donne 8
C'est l'œuf à double germe éclos sous l'arbre de Lydie.

ODE NUMBER 8

Sails burnt,
I'm here where the worlds give way, at the mercy of dogs, turned into a
     god in some sense, to shoulder the vault
Where missiles sometimes collide with a fragment of roofing,
A palace of Rome swept away, a strand of Ophelia's hair.
Those who spawn by night, who sprout on star-droppings,
Later croak in the shelter of burdocks and war drums.
On the road into Egypt you'll hear this braying;
And the breath of the long distance runner, I still draw it in
At the mouth of infernal caverns.
Here the emperor of the three worlds invites me to drink this reek, the
     eternal feminine clotting and pearling.
The water of caves, the striated conch, and the bow
Where nude Diana is aiming her body—and later I see her fresh from
     her Holland bath,
Dressed in jute   The water comes back on the marsh,
It creates an eternity on the transparent lobe.

Also the ass was a hive, where the bees fed on artemisia.

The door opens, we come on the wedding in the wooden bucket foaming
     with soap.
The crow scatters the passion-linen over the meadows: "Oh sun," said I,
     "dry out this crescent of bread
For huntress Diana coming back to her bath."
I had got to the emerald green because of the sea, which had nourished
     me for so long,
The tarred logs under the gulls' feet had lost the blond humour the
     loggers grow drunk on.
Following the snail on the leaf I counted the spires one by one, at the
     same time how many curved beams went to lay the ship *Argo*'s keel.
That part of God which governs the uneven numbers added on to the
     figure for man gives 8
It's the double-yolked egg hatched under the Lydian tree.

Ceints de flanelle rouge les hommes circulaient dans le bruit des machines à battre;
Le duvet des chardons poudrait leur casquette tandis que les femmes en sarrau à fleurs passaient avec des cafetières de Delft servir le fil-en-trois.
Bruit de pattes, coups de bec: les dieux picoraient les graines du fronton
Et l'enfant conçu dans nos greniers prit le lait qu'à l'ordinaire on mesure au décalitre.

Amon à tête de bélier régnait-il sur l'Olympe?
Le roseau fleurissait depuis le commencement
Et vous écoutiez le chant de ce rossignol
Qu'on a épinglé un soir sur la roseraie.
Une île émerge, et l'autre. Une marée de semence envahit le labour. Les bouvillons castrés ahanent dans le crépuscule
Et nous chargés de géraniums—dans la nuit.
A qui oserai-je répondre que nous avons au ciel racine? Ce peu de sable entre mes mains ne garde trace d'aucun pas.
Songe à cette nuit d'été où la Grèce vint faner le foin dans la clairière. Est-ce Avallon qui s'en va avec le voile de la mariée?
Épars partout dans le tumulte,
Et le soleil navigue en vain le zodiaque, et le désir de l'amant dévoile en vain les hanches de la Reine de Saba.
Dieux, et toi-même, mon Dieu, l'éther vous a tués,
Et vous n'êtes plus dans la vitrine que des insectes peu visibles.
Parlez,
Vous qui fûtes témoins,
Et qui retenez entre vos doigts le pétale flambé
D'une rose éteinte par magie.

Féroces vendeurs de pioches, rien pour vous!
Je ne parle qu'aux morts, —à l'Osiris vert.

Un pays d'aires désertées, une pâmoison de mule, voilà mon chant.
D'une guerre d'oiseaux reste la flèche noire dans le gosier du merle. Il y eut de beaux mois de lente tristesse où l'on vannait la récolte; le peuplier n'en finissait pas de se regarder dans l'eau.

Girt about with red flannel the men were moving around in the noise of
the threshing machines;
The thistle down powdered their caps, while flowery-smocked women
with Delft *cafetières* came to serve out the grog.
Beak-blows, feet landing: the gods were pecking the seeds from the
pediment
And the child conceived in our granaries took the milk we usually
measure out by the gallon.

Was ram's-headed Ammon reigning on Olympus?
The reed had flourished since the beginning
And you often heard the song of that nightingale
They pinned one evening out on the rose hedge.
One island emerges, and then the other. A tide of seed floods the tillage.
The castrated bullocks toil on in the twilight
And we, laden down with geraniums—into the night.
To whom will I dare respond that we are rooted in heaven? This bit of
sand in my palms keeps no trace of a footprint.
Think of that midsummer's night when Greece came to toss the hay in
the clearing. Is that Avalon going off with the bridal veil?
Scattered everywhere in the tumult,
In vain the sun sails the Zodiac, and in vain the lover's longing unveils
the hips of the Queen of Sheba.
Gods, and yourself, my God, the ether has slain you,
You're like almost invisible insects in the display case.
Speak,
You who were witnesses,
Whose fingers still hold the scorched petals
Of a rose extinguished by magic.

Nothing for you, brutal pickaxe salesmen!
I speak to the dead alone—to the green Osiris.

A land of deserted threshing floors, mules fainting away, these make
my song.
The black arrow of some bird-battle still sticks in the blackbird's throat.
There were lovely months of slow sadness while they winnowed the
crops; the poplar never left off gazing down at itself in the water.

Inaccessible au marin la mer imprègne les lettres bleues que déchiffre
une femme fécondée. Ah tu lis maintenant la route dans le réseau
de veines que l'iode et le lait parcourent afin de rouler la pelote
qu'Ariane crédule serre entre ses cuisses dans Naxos. Amsterdam
aussi voit ce monde qu'un orage à Venise foudroie. L'amande caille
ici dans le linge, là-bas c'est toute la cartographie de la rosée dans
une coquille close où Compostelle prend chemin. Je n'en finirai
pas de parler de vous mer verte issue de la cornée. Le coquelicot
que n'a pas encore écarté le doigt d'une fille, ovoïde bouton où le
feu en frange est plié, le coquelicot est là, ferme paraphe d'un livre
muet, porte close d'un jardin sans clôture. Le plâtre allégorique
ensemence la lisière et d'un balcon pour chasse à courre j'écoute
le cor de chasse dans la vapeur d'un soir qui s'incline vers l'horizon
où la fermière accroupie à traire en sa main tient le pis d'une vache.
Certainement les mouettes revinrent malgré le vernis qui défend l'âme
de l'hiver. Elles se battirent sur le quai pour une carcasse de hareng.
Ainsi plumes se prennent aux robes des régentes qui gouvernent les
voiliers. Le graillon me chasse vers la Giudecca.
Érudits en violettes: Homère, Pindare et Sappho.
Retournés les boyaux de la mer, c'est le bois de mai
d'où revient l'enfant divin mal dépris des muqueuses
un veau quoi ou tout comme
qui bouche le vagin un moment
pend puis sur la paille est tout gras
au-dessous du délivre. Reines
célestes qui enfantez dans l'herbe et les buissons
et de votre souffle embuez la peinture maniériste
avec vous je couche et certes
cela blesse le cœur qui ne se connaît qu'immortel.
Sur la source sacrée la laiterie s'érige
et sépare en blondeurs pulsées par les Diesels
de nordiques nattes maintenant défaites à l'orée du bois
où les chevillards armés de blancs filets
s'emparent d'aubes et de prêtrises.

Vois pourtant qu'Elle porte la double sphère et l'arceau des cornes; et le
sable fin dont elles polissent sa peau est celui du blason, —noire
matière que les forgerons recueillent dans les îles soulevées par
le feu.

The sea no sailor can reach impregnates blue letters read by a woman heavy with child. Now you're reading the road in the network of veins that the milk and iodine follow to roll up the ball of thread clasped by credulous Ariadne's thighs on Naxos. Amsterdam, too, sees this world lit up by a lightning storm over Venice. Here the almond clots in the linen, there all the cartography of the dew lies in the closed cockleshell where Compostela sets forth. Nor could I ever mirror the verdant ocean issued from the cornea. The poppy that no girl's finger has opened, the ovoid bud folding in the fringed fire—the poppy is there, firm flourish of a mute book, closed door of an unwalled garden. The allegorical statue is casting its seed at the wood's edge, and from a hunting-gallery I can hear the hunter's horn through the misty dusk that slants toward the horizon where the farmwife, crouched to her milking, grasps the udder.

Of course the seagulls came back, in spite of the varnish protecting the soul against winter. They fought on the pier for a herring carcass. Thus feathers catch on the gowns of the Regents who govern the ships. The smell of burnt fat drives me toward the Giudecca.

Deeply learnèd in violets: Homer, Pindar and Sappho.
The sea's bowels heave over, and out of this wood in May
the holy child returns, half detached from the membranes
what, a calf or just like
what blocks the vagina a moment just
hangs then lies greasy there on the straw
under the afterbirth. Celestial
queens who give birth in the bushes and grass
whose breath clouds the mannerist paintings
I come to your bed and indeed this wounds
the heart which only knows itself as immortal.
On the sacred spring the dairy barn rises
and Diesels pulse out the blond hues
of Nordic braids now undone at the edge of the forest
where the butcher's men armed with white nets
seize the vestments and holy orders.

But see how She bears the double sphere and the crescent of horns; the fine sand the women polish her skin with comes from the blazon— black matter gathered by blacksmiths in islands flung up by fire.

L'amant se fait pareil au songe et se colore de chaux;

La lumière le sépare, et battre le taillis ne lève que souvenir de ce qui fut chair révélée. Qu'il presse contre l'écorce le muscle même de son cœur, qu'il déchiffre ensuite les marques laissées,

douleur et sang voilà tout ce qui reste, mais l'omphalos,

mais le grain qu'elle porte à l'aine, il ne les touche plus.

Moisson de mousse, néflier que les chèvres râpent,

tête de chien livrée aux fourmis, c'est qu'il va,

et voyant autre chose voit cela autrement que le boucher.

Elle n'est plus que l'orient d'une perle

Et sur l'Evangile de Jean le premier rayon déjà n'est plus.

Le sacerdoce n'est pas transmis. Ou bien par voie secrète

Artérielle pulsation dans les parages d'une ombrelle rouge

Ouverte sur le versant.

Mille miroirs se déplacent entre le fagot et le chien et les neiges nacrées abolissent à la fin ce qui tant nous meurtrit.

Un renâclement de chevaux sur la planète froide; plus bas l'anguille échappe aux cendres nocturnes, bouge dans les joncs, gagne les bassins de radoub;

Et l'avoine glisse entre les planches, la nuit, quand les maisons aveuglées s'abandonnent à la biologie.

La racine travaille dans le trou. Le pénis du hongre est une vieille comète pendue entre les coffres.

Vous avez eu tort de renier la magie blanche, de dénigrer l'héritage et de jeter dans le puits les douze clés.

Ils avaient tendu la voile violette et le mât décrivait autour de l'étoile ce cône qui permet au quadrige d'entrer après le voyage dans de nouvelles écuries.

Il ôta la peau de mouton qui lui couvrait les épaules, et la pendit au clou de fer. Comme d'autres éteignent une lanterne en soufflant sur la flamme par son souffle il alluma celle-ci.

Il faisait ce printemps pâle que Florence a copié. —Muses!

Le même voile qui vous dérobe à nos yeux dérobe le monde même où nous avions à vivre.

The lover makes himself dreamlike, washes himself white as lime;
The light divides him, and beating the woods only raises the memory of
that which was flesh revealed. Let him press his heart's very muscle
into the bark, and decipher the marks that it leaves,
pain and blood, that's what's left, and yet the omphalos,
and yet the mole that she bears on her groin, he no longer can touch
them.
Harvest of moss, medlar tree fretted by goats,
dog's head left out for the ants, it's because he is going
and sees something else, and so sees this differently than the butcher.

Now she is only the limpid water of a pearl
And already the first ray of sunrise has left the Gospel of John.
The vocation is not passed on. Or only by secret ways
Arterial pulsing about the rim of a red parasol
Opened up on the hillside.
A thousand mirrors are moving between the bundle of twigs and the
dog, and the pearly snows at last put an end to whatever bruised
us so badly.
Horses snorting on the cold planet; lower down the eel escapes from the
nocturnal ashes, moves through the reeds, and comes into the dry
docks;
And the oats slip between the planks, at night, when the blind houses
give themselves up to biology.
The root works in the hole. The gelding's penis hangs like an ancient
comet between the coffers.
You were wrong to abjure white magic, to denigrate the heritage, flinging
the twelve keys down the well.
They had spread the violet sail, and around the star the mast traced the
cone which draws the quadriga into new stables after the journey.
He took off the sheepskin that covered his shoulders and hung it up on
the iron nail. As others blowing blow out a lantern's flame so he
lit this one with his breath.
He was making this pale springtime that Florence has copied.—Muses!
The same veil that hides you away from our eyes hides the very world
we needed to live in.

Je me souviens de toi monstre lithique
Tu broutais la haie au nez du cantonnier
Nous avions laissé derrière les blondes touffeurs du Titien
Sur un lit que les amants avaient taché
Le bouc entre ses babines tenait une jonquille
Que des femmes naviguant le Nil sur une jonque
Essayaient du lui ôter. En vain tu interroges
Le bulletin météorologique : on nous frustre
Du beau temps. La touffe que tu portes
O fille à la naissance du ventre
Tire tu le sais de l'abîme la musique.

Vêtus de cuir vinrent les lyriques,
Nautonniers, matelots. Abattu
Le taureau tombe dans le feuillage. Jugulé
Il laboure le terrain où paissent les brebis.
Un cahotement de charrette. Des travaux d'essartage. Un poète grec
Courtise une bergère mal chaussée. La palpitation des élytres dans l'air
        bleu, la sueur amoureuse, le suint des moutons, la poussière rouge
        des briques, une voile en bas poissée par les doigts des pêcheurs,
        le linge ourlé en bordure du golfe.
Ses cris titubent. Il voit des noces.
Il voit des amants qui sont des amas d'étoiles.
L'ambre coule dans la mer, une fille enfantée
Aborde au rivage armée de lys. A gauche
L'ange de Simone Martini recueille sur la plage le calice.
D'un vol de libellule il raye la mer et le pré.
Un pré de sauge, loin, c'est la nuit, quand à l'ouest l'assemblée des
        scieurs de long—surineurs parfois s'il y a des règlements de compte
        à cause de la paye—de la gamelle d'étain tire la soupe compacte.
Madriers, charpentes équarries parmi le blond chantier : de chaque pièce
        le cube est écrit sur la section au crayon à bois.
Ils vont le dimanche dans les métairies acheter des chèvres,
Et prennent debout les vendeuses de vin enivrées par la sciure et la
        résine.

I remember you, lithic monster
Grazing the hedgerow under the roadmender's nose
We had left Titian's warm blond bushiness behind us
On a bed stained by lovers
Between its pendulous lips the goat held a jonquil
Which women sailing a junk down the Nile
Kept trying to seize. No use your consulting
The weather forecast: they've cut us off
From fine weather. The wisp that you bear
Girl where your belly begins
Draws and you know it music from the abyss.

The lyric poets arrived dressed in leather,
Pilots and sailors. The broken
Bull sinks down in the leaves. Subdued to the yoke,
He ploughs up the land where the sheep are grazing.
A jolting cart. A clearing of ground. A Greek poet
Pays court to an ill-shod shepherdess. Wing-cases throbbing in the blue
    air, the amorous sweat, the sheep grease, red brick-dust, and below,
    a sail sticky with pitch from the fishermen's fingers, the linen
    hemmed on the edge of the gulf.
His cries stagger on. He sees weddings.
He sees lovers, those clusters of stars.
The amber flows into the sea, the newly begotten
Daughter armed with lilies touches the shore. To the left
Simone Martini's angel takes up the chalice.
With a dragonfly's flight he streaks the meadow and sea.
A distant sage field, it's nighttime, when to the west the men from the
    sawyards assemble—cutthroats at times when there are brawls
    because of the pay—and draw the dense soup from the tin mess-
    pan.
Timbers, square-cornered frames in the blond construction: the cube
    of each piece is pencilled out on the section.
On Sundays they go out to the farmstead to buy goats,
And the women selling wine grow drunk on the resin and shavings, and
    they take them there standing up.

Puis ils regardent partir le vaisseau
Dont l'œil peint sur la proue
Scrute la sphère à Hermès dédiée.

Nous n'avons plus pour soleil que ce chaudron de cuivre qui maintient
    un rien de lumière rouge à travers la saison.
De grandes femmes en sarrau remplissent les boudins.
Hérissées d'aiguilles de genévrier elles offrent au ciel leurs entonnoirs
    de fer. Les porcs réclament une part de couenne. Tout est gras et
    froid, et la nuit tombe vite.
La caravane bleue des gardes gagne la Colchide. D'un claquement de
    fouet les muletiers enlèvent l'attelage bruissant de grelots. Taureau
    mort, tronc dépouillé: ils furent marqués vivants, et maintenant ils
    passent la ligne.

Je n'épuise pas les masques. Patiemment je renouvelle sur la figure du
    dieu la semblance fausse où l'oronge dévore un abominable lupus.
    Viens, mangeuse de cerises,
Avant que la coquille se referme, avant que les millions de taches de la
    panthère brûlent ta beauté. Savante en vénerie laisse qu'en tes
    veines je poursuive ma proie;
Laisse-moi coucher dans ce lacis où le fauve s'étrangle à tirer sur la
    viorne. Laisse! J'assemble la meute, je brise la mémoire.
Que tout un pan de toi pourrisse à l'endroit du monde où la mer se retire
Et la torche s'avive qui plaque de ses lueurs sur la houille
L'offrande ancienne et l'ancien don.
De la pierre déliant une chasse que la poix sur le hallier projette,
Par combats vers toi j'occupe des terres après la jacinthe et le chiendent.
Ne chois pas sous les plumets de l'orage
Avant que l'époux au long pénis te féconde: —il a déjà là-bas ton lit
    prêt dans le tulle vert
Où cillent les planètes.

Then they watch the ship as it leaves.
The eye painted on its prow
Scans the sphere dedicated to Hermes.

Now all we have for a sun is the copper cauldron holding its faint ruddy
    light through the season.
Vast women in smocks are stuffing the sausages.
Bristling with juniper needles they lift their meat funnels up to the sky.
    The pigs claim their share of the pork-rind. Everything's greasy
    and cold, and the night comes down quickly.
The blue caravan of the guards comes to Colchis. With a crack of their
    whip, the drovers urge on the mule team sounding with bells. Dead
    bull, trunk stripped bare: they were marked while alive, and now
    they pass over the line.

I can never exhaust the masks. Patiently over the god's face I renew the
    false appearance of a poisonous mushroom devouring the features
    riddled with lupus. Come, cherry-stained mouth,
Before the shell closes again, before thousands of leopard-spots scorch
    your beauty. Mistress of hunting, let me pursue my prey through
    your veins;
Let me lie down in this tangle where wild things are strangled leaping
    against the clematis. Only let me! I'll shatter memory, assemble
    the pack.
May a whole part of you rot at that point in the world where the sea is
    withdrawing
And the torch revive whose gleams fling up on the coal
The ancient offering, the ancient gift.
Unwinding out of the stone a hunt which the pitch projects onto the
    thicket,
Through combats towards you I occupy lands just after the wheat-grass
    and bluebells.
Do not sink beneath the storm's plumes
Before the husband's long penis has quickened your body: already he
    has prepared your bed in the deep green tulle
Where the planets flicker.

III

FROM
Sibylles
(1971)

CIRCE

POUR MIODRAG PAVLOVITCH

Avec leur fourche
ils ont tourné sur son lit le brasier
vers quoi l'ânesse brait derrière les lauriers-roses

et la mouette au bec rose
déchire la couenne cuite des cochons.
Minuit
le minotaure vous étend sur la braise
mariée blanche
comme la crique d'un défunt miroir
où les naufrages soudain reparaissent
quand les chiens guettent sur la rive
le décennal retour.

La pourpre va jaillir
avec, le poséidonien trône
et la reine au ventre fendu d'un délicat couteau
aux aines deux spirales peintes comme trompes
de papillons abreuvés la nuit de violettes.

Racontez-moi la mort
la résurrection d'Aphrodite
parmi les valves et pédoncules de palourdes
dans l'onctueux sperme de l'étalon
qui des quatre fers étoile la nocturne route.

Dites-moi le nom des poissons, des entrailles
sur la trace du soldat serbe
et jusqu'au troyen repaire
de l'amante constellée. Je n'aurai plus
que l'unique parole à confier au bûcheron
à la tisseuse de toile
d'un seul fil fixant le vautour et la danse
le chevreau à son outre lactée
à la figue une guêpe noire et jaune
dont la cire fausse noircira les autels.

⌒CIRCE

FOR MIODRAG PAVLOVITCH

With their pitchfork
they've stirred up the blazing bed of coals
while the she-ass brays behind the rose-laurels

and the seagull
tears at a porkrind with its rosy beak.
Midnight
the minotaur stretches you out on the embers
white bride
like the inlet in a dead mirror
where shipwrecks suddenly reappear
while the dogs on the shore await
the tenth-year return.

The purple will flood outward
with it, the throne of Poseidon
and the queen's belly slit with a delicate blade
and her groin with its two painted spirals like horns
of butterflies drenched by violets in the night.

Tell me the death
the rebirth of Aphrodite
among the muscles and valves of clams
in the oily sperm of the stallion
whose iron heels leave stars on the midnight road.

Tell me the name of the fish, of the guts
on the Serb soldier's track
all the way to the Trojan lair
of the starry beloved. Then I will have
only the word itself to offer the woodman
or the weaving woman who holds
with a single strand the vulture and the dance
and the kid to its milky jug
and on the fig one black and yellow wasp
darkening the altar with false wax.

Soùs les chênes
dispersez la troupe porcine, servantes
tandis que des plantes tinctoriales
votre maîtresse extrait le jus
et du pavot l'amère confiture.
Sous le gras soleil, matelots
et pirates même à bannière de scorpion
quadrillent le terrain
comme un échiquier
maintenant où toute bête fouaille.
(Les morceaux de mer entrevus
ne seront que tessons dans l'anfractuosité des roches.
Ballottés dans la soue, on vous entend
comme satisfaits.)

Noirs cierges sur la blanche nécropole! Il ne reste
qu'une coquille aux mains de la plaisance
et la musique défaite ourle l'ouïe
ou bien les volutes d'un gosier. Buffles lents
bœufs assoupis, c'est le bois, c'est la brique
qui transhument par les chemins pigmentés d'ocre
ce sont les charrettes lentement dévorées
par le feu. Intestinale paix au long des rives
plus de jeux autour des catafalques, plus de dais
à l'entrée des vignobles. Plus de pieds essuyés
plus de parfums. Plus d'huile douce
dans les chevelures. Plus de vierge volée

et la mer est sans taureau
et le grand dieu de l'éveil a quitté le bulbe
et sans huile la dame s'étiole.
Tout est pareil cependant, mais à quoi?
Le jeu fonctionne. Les fous
ont tué la cavalerie. Le roi pourrit
sans fin dans les latrines.

Qu'à la table du menuisier
une fois de plus la myrtille vous barbouille
ailés, musiciens du pôle

Beneath the oaks
scatter the drove of swine, handmaidens
while your mistress extracts
the juice of dye-bearing plants
and the sour jam of the poppy.
Under a greasy sun, the sailors
and even the pirates with scorpion banners
quadrille the ground
like a chessboard
where every last beast now is grunting.
(Glimpsed fragments of sea
will only be shards in the clefts of the rocks.
As you bob about in the pigsty, one senses
you are content.)

Black tapers on the white necropolis! Only a shell remains
in the hands of the Sunday sailors
and the music, undone, hems at our hearing
or at the scrolls of a throat. Sluggish bisons,
dazed bulls, it is the wood, the brick
drifting like flocks up the ochre-stained roads
it is the great carts slowly devoured
by flames. Intestinal peace along the shores
no more games by the catafalque, no canopy
at the vineyard's entrance. No wiping of feet
or perfumes. No sweet oil
in the hair. No more stolen virgins

and the sea has lost its bull
and the great god of waking has fled the bulb
and without her oil the lady has grown pale.
Still everything reminds us, but of what?
The game still functions. The madmen
have slaughtered the cavalry. The king
rots endlessly in the latrines.

At the joiner's table
may the dark berries stain you once more
winged men, musicians of the pole

qui par la corne où les oiseaux se posent
dès le matin assemblez les Muses
détournant ainsi de l'aire la mutinerie

et le chœur
tout à sa clameur consacré aspire
et souffle
pour qu'il émerge du lierre vendangé
celui qui n'est pas sourd au silence des morts
et la source
qu'autrefois le puits contenait
soudain préfère les cordes émouvoir
et les hanches d'une femme ornée
d'un bracelet de perles, que la danse mêle
aux germes, aux graines, au pétillement
de la paille quand les granges s'anuitent
alors
les coureuses de hardes, au-dessus de l'herbe
un pied suspendu
entre leurs seins regardent la sueur couler
rosée qui goutte à goutte descend
de la lune jusqu'au rosier.

Arbustes, l'églantine enneige leur peau, le vent
pique là ses échardes, incendiant le sacre
les dieux se taisent, l'olivier compta
siècles et millénaires sur la pierre
et le four à pain rougeoie quand la chouette
d'un poudroiement de plumes décide
d'embaumer la nuit. Le troupeau vaque
les oreilles tendues vers l'abreuvoir
le grand silence est sur la terre
Eros est un loup, César
la seule image sanctifiante
où donc
ont sombré les villes? Je n'entends même plus
l'oxydation des édifices, le gloussement du mazout
dans les artères, le grésillement
de l'électricité dans les câbles, le s o s

who all morning assemble the Muses
by the horn where birds alight
thus turning away the mutiny from this ground

and the choir
all to its outcry devoted, aspires
and breathes
so that he who hears the silence of the dead
·may emerge from the gathered ivy
and the spring
once enclosed by the well
suddenly prefers to sway the ropes
and the hips of a woman adorned
with an armlet of pearls, which the dance
mingles with seeds, with buds, with the rustle
of straw as night comes down on the barns
then
the wild huntresses running with one foot suspended
over the grass
watch the sweat run trickling between their breasts
dew falling drop by drop
from the moon to the rose-tree.

Shrubs, the eglantine snowdrifts their skin, the wind
stirs up its thistles, kindling the sacrament
the gods fall silent, the olive tree counted
centuries and millennia on the rock
and the bread-oven reddens as the screech owl
decides to perfume the night
with his powdery plumes. The herd wanders vacantly
ears pricked to the watering place
great silence is on the earth
Eros is a wolf, Caesar
the only sanctifying image
then where
did the cities founder? I no longer hear
even the buildings corroding, the clunking of oil
in the arteries, electricity
crackling through cables or the S.O.S.

des téléphonistes flambant avec leur jupe
de nylon et le hauturier réseau
dont les mailles leur coupent la carotide.

Ayant gravi les degrés du temple
l'Inca voit à ses pieds le serpent reformer la boucle
et l'uræus sur l'autre rive descend du frontal
pour gonfler de nouveau son buccal abcès
et de spasmes en agonie
il ingurgite la race autrefois graciée

avance la veuve ornée de mauves
les chevilles entravées de liseron
un dernier derrick
pompe la salive bleue du désert
les chevaux qu'on avait oubliés sous le harnais
tirent vers la coupe de lave l'ultime piano

mais le chœur
tout à l'extase occupé
veut (portant tous ses vœux à ne pas vouloir)
conduire son souffle
par le réseau même que le sang irrigue
briser le basalte
où le germe fut le huitième jour enseveli
il accomplit le rite intérieur de la purification
détourne de leur voie les liquides
par l'échelle d'os et de moelle
atteint le toit crêté
où le pigeon se pose
après avoir dévié de l'horizon son aile

alors les visages des divins tentent d'émerger
en transparence entrevus
le front peint, les femelles
leur pubis offrant la convexe conque au lotus
leur ventre au labyrinthe
et l'attache du cou ponctuée de pluie

of the operators flaming in their nylon
skirts and the deepsea network
whose meshes sever their carotid.

Having scaled the temple steps, the Inca
sees the snake at his feet reforming the loop
and on the far shore the sacred asp descends
from the brow again to swell his abscessed cheek
and with agonized spasms
devours the race that once had known reprieve

now the widow in her mallows comes
her ankles bound with flowering vines
one last derrick
pumps the blue saliva from the desert
the horses forgotten in harness pull
the last piano toward the lava cup

but the choir
all busy with its ecstasy
wants (exerting all of its will against wanting)
to guide its breath
through the very network the blood irrigates
to shatter the basalt
where the seed on the eighth day was buried
it fulfills the inner, purifying rite
turns the fluids from their course
by the bone-and-marrow ladder
and reaches the crested roof
where the pigeon alights
after swerving its wing away from the horizon

then the divine faces try to emerge
glimpsed in transparency
the painted brow, the females
whose delta offers a convex shell to the lotus
their belly to the labyrinth
and the base of the neck punctuated by rain

lacrimae Virginis, Maris stellae
n'approchez pas, très belles
ne coupez pas vos doigts
au fer-blanc des conserveries
moins que toute autre, vous
insulaire Ariane
que le dieu avait élue
et qui êtes la sainte
que les toreros vénèrent
dans la chapelle des places

icône vacillante à la flamme d'un cierge
alors tout prend ce goût d'abeille dans l'acacia
que les adolescents connaissent
au déclin de l'après-midi.

D'un coup de hache
le vide s'engouffre au-dessous du diaphragme
et c'est la rose pourprée
qui maintenant de sa langue
palpe le péritoine
dans la vacuité angélique

quand l'air plein de braise peigne
jusqu'à l'ombre des ruisseaux
ses longues boucles slaves

STELE

pour l'âne dont les cartilages
fleurissent le fossé
pour le chien, pour l'enfant
qui refroidit sous ma paume
dans l'herbe rase de l'Europe
je revois tes pieds nus
qu'un peu de sang tache
et ta robe gitane

lacrimae Virginis, Maris stellae
beautiful forms, don't come nearer
don't cut your fingers
on the canneries' tin
and you least of all
island Ariadne
whom the god had chosen
and who are the saint
the toreros venerate
in the chapel of the bullrings

icon swaying in a taper's flame
while everything takes just one bee-sip in the acacia
which the adolescents know
in the afternoon's decline.

Like an axe-blow
the void gusts down under the diaphragm
and now it's the purpled rose
whose tongue explores
the peritoneum
in angelic vacancy

while the air full of embers combs
into the shadow of streams
its long slavonic curls

STELE

for the ass whose gristle
flowers the ditch
for the dog, for the child
grown cold beneath my palm
in the smooth grass of Europe
again I see your bare feet
stained with a little blood
and your gypsy dress

et ton épaule tachée de framboise
où l'aile lentement pousse son duvet noir

ainsi la beauté de l'oiseau et celle de la renarde
ici succombent
dans le chuintement de la gomme sur l'asphalte

aucun dieu ne vient

notre Père qui êtes aux cieux
que votre règne arrive
seulement la brute habillée de vinyl
qui disperse à coups de mâchoires
le chœur lamentable
nul sacre ni sacrement
le monde n'est qu'un tas de faits divers
la mort au visage de chevrotines
s'avance parmi nous
incognito, saccageant en nuits de noces
la lingerie des motels

les pauvres n'ont plus de larmes
depuis qu'on gouverne en leur nom

privés de parole, absents de toute prière
ils vont
nippés de surplus, persuadés
de n'être rien d'autre que ce qu'ils sont.

Je dis: rien n'est tragique
depuis que le crâne de l'homme
a perdu la forme du ciel
je dis
et vous me maudissez
bénédiction d'Eve sur le trésor

je dis à l'ange
tu es Thot, tu es Hermès
les serpents t'obéissent—et le calame.

and the raspberry stain of your shoulder, where slowly
the wing puts forth its dark down

so the beauty of birds and vixens
perishes here
in the screeching of rubber on asphalt

and no god comes

our Father which art in heaven
thy kingdom come
only the brute dressed in vinyl
whose jawing scatters
the sorrowful choir
no consecration, no sacrament
the world is only a pile of tabloid news
the buckshot face of death
moves among us
incognito, ransacking on wedding nights
the motel linen

the poor have no more tears
since we govern in their name

wordless, absent from all prayer
they go about
decked out in surplus, persuaded
they're nothing more than what they are.

I say: nothing is tragic
since the skull of man
has lost the form of heaven
I say
and you curse me
Eve's blessing on the treasure

I say to the angel
you are Thoth, you are Hermes
the serpents obey you—and the reed.

IV

FROM
*Traité du blanc et
des teintures*
(1978)

⌒*FROM* TRAITE DU BLANC ET DES TEINTURES

Un feu aux basses combes des vendées!
Soudain ce goût de pomme
et l'arbre dressé dans le milieu du monde
quand les eaux font aux lunes contrepoids
et qu'ont fleuri les branches coronaires.

Venez, Vénus, tendre au fleuve vos cheveux,
vous qu'une conque a échouée
où nul ne vous contemple.
L'unique lacs, à vous de le dénouer
afin que mesure l'arbre
le désir même s'érigeant en murmure.

Ici le lait se coagule
qui met au monde les galaxies,
vers le jardin la licorne court
dont l'ivoire du front
touche à l'aine la dame assise.

Double, le serpent paraît
de part et d'autre du tronc. Un oiseau
se détache, et brûlant sur son erre
plus haut reprend
sa haute errance.

A chaque arceau se déplie un soleil,
degrés que l'humus convoite
d'une échelle où déjà le volubilis
déchiffre par volutes
la trajectoire et l'accès.

Le monde encore n'a qu'une voix,
mais l'onde propagée
en s'éloignant du point s'appesantit,

FROM TREATISE ON WHITE
AND THE TINCTURES

A fire in the low combes of the vendées!
Suddenly this tang of apples
and the tree drawn up in the midst of the world
while the waters counterpoise the moons
and the coronary branches are blooming.

Come, Venus, spread out your hair to the river,
a shell has stranded you far
from all contemplation.
Only one knot, and only you to undo it
so that desire itself
rising up in a murmur may measure the tree.

The milk which brings forth
the galaxies clots here,
and the unicorn running toward the garden
touches his ivory
to the seated lady's groin.

Double, the serpent appears
around both sides of the trunk. A bird
flaps away, and flaming over its aerial
range, resumes
its swaying still higher.

At each arch a sun unfurls,
and the humus longs for the rungs
of this ladder where whorls
of morning glory already decipher
the trajectory and access.

As yet the world has only one voice,
but the propagated wave
in moving away from the point grows heavy,

d'un effluve formant le fleuve
ainsi que tous états
selon fréquence et amplitude.

Par la verticale
ici se scinde l'autre sel,
unique larme des dieux,
car après tout est vie, mort et saisons.
De la bourbe le saturnien surgit
avec l'aquatique sirène
en un même ovale miroir qui regardent
le feu premier et la terre promise.

Ils te voient, archange à l'épée de nitre.
Ils te voient, impératrice des étoiles,
vierge maritime, océane licorne.
Ils t'entendent,
Père qui êtes aux cieux.

Lui, d'une pomme coupée à l'équateur
où flambe l'étoile pentagone,
offre les deux parts
et la pulpe angiosperme
ouverte à l'un et l'autre pôle.

Le ciel vacille sur sa tige,
l'averse profère le printemps,
un parfum de feuilles
traîne sur les eaux. L'ombre déjà
et la couleur teignent les rais de la roue.

Une seule boucle un instant
enclôt la flèche avec l'archer,
les branches frémissent,
et le sillon
que fait la pluie sous le pêcher.

L'image en un même miroir
se dédouble et connaît de ses rives
ce qui tremble,

from effluvia forming the river
as well as all states
according to amplitude and frequency.

Through the vertical
the other salt here divides,
the gods' single tear,
for after all is life, death, and the seasons.
From the mire the Saturnian surges
beside the watery siren
beholding in one oval mirror
the primal fire and promised land.

They see you, archangel with the nitre sword.
Starry empress, they see you,
oceanic unicorn, maritime virgin.
They hear you,
Father who art in heaven.

He, of an apple sliced
across the equator and blazed with the five-pointed star,
holds out the two parts
and the crisp flesh surrounding
the seedcase and pierced at both poles.

The sky sways on its stem,
a shower utters its springtime,
a leafy fragrance
trails on the waters. Already the shadow
and colors tincture the spokes of the wheel.

For one instant a single loop
encloses archer and arrow,
the branches quiver,
and the furrow
of rain running under the peach tree.

In one mirror the image
doubles, and knows of its banks
whatever is trembling,

le bruit labile des sources
que la spirale dédoublée
pulse plus haut.

En lèvres et labelles
l'onde pliée palpite,
déjoue la chute, au gosier
jubile, dans la coquille,
dans le jeu des genoux.

L'anneau qu'ils forment maintenant s'ouvre
et ce qu'ils voient c'est la sphère encore
pareille au paon, l'oiseau lourd d'œillets,
dont ils accueillent la jalouse alarme
au bord béant des mers.

En eux le même ressac!
Nés de l'algue et du gel des nostocs,
issus des peuplements de gorgonies,
des ramures cœliaques,
à peine au premier souffle qu'ils aspirent
leur revient la souvenance viscérale.

Où s'épand le phosphore du poulpe
ils configurent des yeux
l'alphabet, et lisent en phylactère
les noms
que l'anse et la croix
font naître dans ce creux.

En eux l'érection de l'arbre,
la pommaison et l'ophidienne phase
où la gorge se peuple de grain.
C'est le temps de la corneille,
c'est avant que les oiseaux s'abecquent.

Connivence de l'éclair et du sacre.
Ecoute au long le halo t'envahir
d'une lampe pareille
au bulbe gorgé de terriennes huiles.

the labile sound of the spring
which the doubled spiral
pulses still higher.

The folded wave
throbs among lips and petals,
it baffles the Fall, and delights
in the throat, in the shell,
and in the play of knees.

Now the ring they form opens out
and they see the sphere still
like the peacock, heavy with eyeletted flowers,
and greet his jealous alarm
at the sea's yawning edge.

And the same surf is in
them! Born of the seaweed, star-jelly,
sprung from the stands of sea-coral,
from the internal branchings,
barely their first breath is drawn
when the visceral memories return.

Where the octopus spreads, phosphorescent
with their eyes they fashion
the alphabet, and they read
the phylactery of names
born in this hollow
to the cross and curved loop.

In them the tree is drawn up
and the apple, ophidian phase,
the throat peopled with grain.
It is the time of the crow,
before the birds begin nesting.

The lightning and sacrament conspire.
Listen steadily as the lamp's
halo invades you, a bulb
gorged with terrestrial oils.

Écoute d'escalade en escalade
l'hélianthe se nourrir,
franchissant les sas,
ouvrant dans l'os
l'inflorescence.

Dormeuse en eau qui brille,
le rayon maintenant l'atteint
et délute mieux chaque orifice
où le chant répond et compose
quelle bulle au calcaire.

Hors des liens la floraison explore
en sinueux parcours la paroi de l'ogive,
ondule
comme dans l'œil la rumeur
d'une prairie au vent de mai.

De l'aster aux lunes éparses
mais que règle quelque cycle
dans l'opaque poids de la chair
chacun de l'autre
froisse la texture.

Croule au pré ce qui fut joint,
au crêt rebrousse le plumail,
clame défaite sur le mât,
s'abat, revient, amasse en gerbe,
s'éjouit de fleurs.

Qu'ils battent le jeu
ne change pas la rotation des lames,
majesté du destin écrite
en vingt-deux lettres
dont n'est tenu le compte
ailleurs que dans la résille courbe
où compute le corbeau.

Listen as the sunflower
draws its life from one height to the next.
Beyond the airlocks
it opens the pattern
of bloom in the bone.

At last the ray reaches her sleep
in the glittering water
and better unseals every inlet
where the chanting responds and composes
bubbles deep in the limestone.

Free from all bonds, the lengths
of sinuous bloom explore
the pointed arch, and wave
in the eye like remote
prairie murmurs in the wind of May.

From the aster to the scattered moons
which some cycle yet rules
in the opaque weight of the flesh
each ruffles
the other's texture.

What was joined together falls back on the meadow,
strokes back the plumes at the helm,
proclaims its defeat from the mast,
hurls down, returns, and gathers in sheaves,
rejoices in flowers.

That they shuffle the game
cannot alter one card's rotation,
fate majestically written
in twenty-two letters
of which no account is kept
except in the vast curving network
computed by crows.

Confuse forêt
voile en eux l'arbre qu'ils recèlent.
Oscille aux crocs l'orchidée,
dans la brèche
l'adamique pomme.

Expulsés, qu'ils se tournent,
partout la distance est égale
de l'espace foulé
à l'innombrable enceinte
que n'embrasse aucun compas.

A confused forest
veils the tree they conceal within.
The orchid sways on its tusks,
and in the gap
the apple of Adam.

Expelled, let them turn and look back,
the distance is everywhere equal
from the space trodden down
to the numberless precinct
no compass can span.

NOTES

⌒NOTES

CHARENTE

(Robert Marteau's note.) In rural France, when a priest is called to administer the last Sacraments to the dying, he carries the Host and is accompanied by a choirboy who rings a small bell, so that those who hear it will know a human creature is about to yield up his soul to God.

LOZERE

Lozère is a wild, bare, mountainous region at the southern end of the Massif Central; English readers may know it as the setting of Robert Louis Stevenson's *Travels with a Donkey*. In the early eighteenth century, a half-legendary wolf—the *Bête de Gevaudan*—terrorized the area, and made a practice of racing stagecoaches.

MELUSINE

The story of Mélusine has its origins in Poitevin folklore. She is that pervasive figure, the fairy who is human above her waist, but at certain times becomes serpentine below. Mélusine's husband, the lord of the château of Lusignan, has sworn never to visit her on Saturday, without knowing the reason for his vow. Eventually, spying on her in her bath (a sort of vat in which she is often depicted), he discovers her secret. She flees, but continues to haunt the château; her wailing is heard in times of trouble for the seigneurs of Lusignan.

FOR THE TWELFTH ANNIVERSARY OF THE DEATH OF MANOLETE

The greatness of the celebrated matador was considered to lie in his restrained and classical capework, in his controlled and courageous guidance of the bull, and in his own almost statue-like immobility.

VERONICA

The Veronica is a pass in which the bull's brow and horns barely brush through the held-out cape; it is named for the napkin with which Saint Veronica wiped the face of Christ on the road to Calvary.

BLACK BANDERILLAS

The barbed, dart-like *banderillas* are planted to animate the bull before he is engaged by the matador. The black *banderillas* are used to correct the bull when he lacks nobility and courage. They create deeper wounds than the others.

FAENA DE CAPA

This Spanish phrase means work with the cape generally, and signifies all the passes made with it.

ODE NUMBER 8

Eight: the number of manifestation, action, conjugation of forces: the spider and the octopus ramifying and reaching out from the central point of creation. The eight-pointed star that guides the Magi towards the Incarnation.

THE LOCKERT LIBRARY OF
POETRY IN TRANSLATION

George Seferis: Collected Poems (1924-1955), translated, edited, and introduced by Edmund Keeley and Philip Sherrard

Collected Poems of Lucio Piccolo, translated and edited by Brian Swann and Ruth Feldman

C. P. Cavafy: Collected Poems, translated by Edmund Keeley and Philip Sherrard and edited by George Savidis

Benny Andersen: Selected Poems, translated by Alexander Taylor

Selected Poetry of Andrea Zanzotto, translated and edited by Ruth Feldman and Brian Swann

Poems of René Char, translated by Mary Ann Caws and Jonathan Griffin

Selected Poems of Tudor Arghezi, translated and edited by Michael Impey and Brian Swann

Tadeusz Różéwicz: "The Survivor" and Other Poems, translated and introduced by Magnus J. Krynski and Robert A. Maguire

"Harsh World" and Other Poems by Ángel González, translated by Donald D. Walsh

Ritsos in Parentheses, translated and with an introduction by Edmund Keeley

LIBRARY OF CONGRESS CATALOGING IN PUBLICATION DATA

Marteau, Robert.
  Salamander.

  (The Lockert library of poetry in translation)
  I. Title.
PQ2673.A75A28 1979   841'.9'14   78-70307
ISBN 0-691-06396-6
ISBN 0-691-01357-8 pbk.